# The
# Adaptable
# Flyfisher

# The Adaptable Flyfisher

## Wild Trout and Coarse Fish on Fly

## Lou Stevens

SWAN·HILL PRESS

Copyright © 2000 Lou Stevens

2nd Edition first published in the UK in 2000
by Swan Hill Press, an imprint of Airlife Publishing Ltd

1st Edition published in 1990 by Blandford

**British Library Cataloguing-in-Publication Data**
A catalogue record for this book
is available from the British Library

ISBN 1 84037 180 3

The information in this book is true and complete to the best of our knowledge. All recommendations are made without any guarantee on the part of the Publisher, who also disclaims any liability incurred in connection with the use of this data or specific details.

Typeset by Phoenix Typesetting, Ilkley, West Yorkshire
Printed in England by St. Edmundsbury Press, Bury St. Edmunds, Suffolk.

# Swan Hill Press
an imprint of Airlife Publishing Ltd
101 Longden Road, Shrewsbury, SY3 9EB, England
E-mail: airlife@airlifebooks.com
Website: www.airlifebooks.com

For Eddie Bassin –
who was much more than just a friend

*By the same author:*
*Trout and Terrestrials (Swan Hill Press)*
*Improve Your Flycasting (Swan Hill Press)*
*Trout and the Subsurface Fly (Swan Hill Press)*
*Flyfishing – Tactics on Small Streams (Swan Hill Press)*

# Contents

# *Introduction*

Like many other anglers, I began my fishing activities at a very early age, visiting and regularly fishing the local ponds for the roach they contained. The welcome present of a flyrod in my early teens changed things dramatically. Trout fishing was not then available to me, so my attention was turned to the challenge of taking coarse fish on a fly. My casting skill was minimal – I was self taught – but coarse fish were plentiful enough, and obliging. On my return from army service, my fishing was once again restricted to coarse fish, but my scope was enlarged as new techniques were learned and my casting improved.

A move to work in Canada and the USA brought the prospect of unlimited trout; they were halcyon days. It was at this point that my angling career came under the influence of Eddie Bassin – a noted North American flyfisher, and an ex-Canadian Casting Champion. Many happy years were spent in the company of Eddie; his endless, tireless instruction was invaluable. It might be thought that the conversion from coarse fish to trout was therefore complete, but not so. Experience in North America only confirmed my view that coarse fish are a very worthwhile quarry for the adaptable flyfisherman and should not be neglected.

Today, although 90 per cent or so of my fishing is for wild trout, many happy days are spent in pursuit of coarse fish on a fly. The angler who appreciates that this sport is available is indeed lucky. The variety is a pleasure in itself, the change of tactics is always exciting, and the enlarged horizon of knowledge is very satisfying. Alas, Eddie Bassin is no longer with us – he now fishes celestial waters – but whenever I am conscious of making a mistake, I still instinctively wait to hear his harsh but accurate words of criticism, delivered in that raucous voice.

It is hoped, through these pages, that the reader will also benefit from the peerless instruction of Eddie, and that coarse fish, on a fly, will complete the serious flyfisher's angling repertoire.

LOU STEVENS

# Chapter 1

# *The Week-end Flyfisherman*

Very few ardent flyfishermen are in the enviable position of living close to good water and being free to fish whenever the fancy takes them. Even fewer are in that ideal position where they own their own water and have unrestricted access.

It matters little how keen we are; many other considerations have to be taken into account. The majority of anglers need to spend good fishing time earning a living, the house has to be maintained, the gardening done, the lawn cut, and so on. Then, of course, the family has to be considered; wife or husband and children cannot be abandoned as soon as fishing conditions look right. Children need to know their father rather better than just the fellow who is forever loading the car with fishing tackle.

So, the enthusiast must take the chances when obligations allow, and each outing will become a special occasion. Perhaps considerable distances may have to be covered before suitable water can be reached, or the fishing restricted to the local reservoir where the scenery never changes. Of course, there are always the holidays to look forward to, but very often these are taken in locations more suitable for the needs of the family, or friends, and good trout fishing is seldom available close to good beaches.

However, if the established reservoir trout fisherman, or the regular coarse fisherman, is prepared to consider river fishing, then the prospects look considerably better. Very few areas of the UK, Europe or North America are without rivers or streams that hold either wild trout or coarse fish. While it is true that the majority of these wild trout are smaller than those encountered when reservoir fishing, no less skill is required to catch them. In fact, the varied tactics that must be employed will act as a refresher course for the angler who has become set in his ways.

Several species of coarse fish are excellent quarry for the flyfisherman. True, they cannot all be expected to grace the table, but the skill required to take them on a fly is a pleasure in itself. It must be remembered that the regular coarse angler does not automatically fish for the pot – the pleasure lies in the catching of the fish. So why not pursue these fish with a fly? It is a delightful way to take them, and it opens up new vistas for the weekend, or holiday, flyfisherman.

In the following pages, I intend to show that the reservoir angler is probably already equipped to pursue wild river trout or coarse fish. The skills required may already be possessed, but here they will be fully covered for the benefit of the novice, and the skilled flyfisherman may welcome the refresher course. He may, perhaps, pick up some new ideas!

For the flyfisherman who is prepared to consider coarse fish as a quarry, there is the added advantage of a prolonged season. Those well-known predators, the pike and perch, are at their best after the trout season has ended. Both are excellent targets for the flyfisherman. Pike on a fly? Yes, why not? It has been an accepted practice for years in northern Canada, where the muskie – and its close relative, the northern pike – are, on average, larger than those found in the UK. Certainly, modified terminal tackle is necessary, and the fly – or, more accurately, the lure – is larger than usual, but both can be easily handled with normal tackle.

However, the pike and perch are not the only coarse fish that can be taken on a fly. At one time or another most coarse fish, other than confirmed bottom-feeders, take the occasional natural fly or terrestrial or aquatic insect as part of their diet. Some of them are regular takers of insect life and will rise quite freely to an artificial offering. Of necessity, the tactics used by the angler will for the coarse species vary from those used to take trout. Each of these fish will be covered in detail, their special needs discussed and full consideration given to the special flies needed for their capture.

It is hoped that the reader already ties his own flies, a rewarding hobby in itself, but if this is not the case, sufficient detail will be given for flies to be ordered from the usual supplier. Flytying, in its simplest form, is not difficult; there are many flytying courses held around the country, or instruction can be obtained from a flytying friend. It cannot be over-emphasised how much more pleasurable it is to catch fish on personally tied flies. Tying flies is a delightful way to spend those hours when not actually fishing; all types of experimentation are possible, and a good stock of flies is always to hand. If you, the reader, do not 'tie-your-own' – at least give it a try.

The wild trout, the 'brownie' of the rivers and streams in the UK, has always been a worthwhile adversary. Today, partly through lack of conservation, partly due to the adverse effect of modern civilisation on the environment, brownies are inclined to be smaller than in years gone by. Pollution, thank goodness, is almost under control, and many of our cleaned-up rivers and streams now support a good trout population. It is ironic that this has come to pass at the very time when angling interest in the rivers is at a low ebb. It is now easy to obtain fishing permission on rivers that not so many years ago were strictly preserved.

There are now more flyfishermen in the UK than ever before, and it is hard to understand this decided lack of interest in river fishing. Without doubt the advent of reservoir fishing has a lot to do with it – many coarse fishermen now regularly flyfish these waters for rainbow trout without giving a thought to the rivers on which they served their apprenticeship. What a great pity! The week-end or holiday angler is in an ideal position to capitalise on this situation. It will open up new horizons, new venues and new species to angle for, and has a shorter close season.

The flyfisherman needs to have an open mind on the species he pursues. The writer, while fishing in the USA and Canada, was amazed at the ingenuity shown. Not only were freshwater bass and sunfish regularly taken on fly, but the southern States had a large contingent of flyfishermen concentrating on salt-water species, often with spectacular results. Perhaps the holiday angler will feel inclined to experiment with our own common mackerel – it all adds to the fun!

So let us, together, examine the possibilities of widening our scope. First, we will review the tackle requirements.

# Chapter 2

# Tackle

It is most difficult to recommend the type of tackle that should be used by anyone. Tackle is a very personal thing, and individual preferences have to be taken into consideration, for whatever suits one person may not suit another. Opinions also differ as to what is correct under any given circumstances, so it would be very wrong for the writer to attempt to foist his personal ideas upon the reader.

Nevertheless, the passage of time and experience has laid down certain guidelines, and it is in the light of these guidelines that advice is offered. The reader should feel free to vary from any advice given if past experience has proved that alternative tackle is better suited to his needs. As an example, for years I have fished with a short split-cane rod weighing only 85 g (3 oz), a rod that would be totally unsuitable for the majority of readers but has proved itself the perfect mate for me.

For general river fishing, other than small streams, especially where flyfishing for coarse fish is involved, the accepted flyrod would be one 2.58 m (8½ ft) in length, either in carbon, fibre glass or bamboo. Today, carbon is widely used, but that does not mean that it is necessarily the best material for a flyrod. It is more expensive than glass and in many cases is more fragile, but carbon rods will normally tolerate a range of flylines, which is a very useful feature. Fibreglass and bamboo rarely have this tolerance, and it is necessary to adhere to the specifications of the makers. A lot has been said in praise of the lighter weight of carbon and fibreglass. Much of this is pure advertising – weight is of minor importance compared to the balance of a rod. A badly-balanced lightweight rod will always feel heavy, whereas a well-balanced rod of heavier weight will be a delight to use.

Apart from weight and feel, the most important features of a rod are the reel seat, the hand-grip, and the rod rings. Various makers have their own favourite reel seating, and most are excellent, but when selecting a rod attention should be paid to the security the system offers. The reel should be held securely, and no movement should be detected in any direction, especially from side to side. The rod handle should offer a good grip and be long enough to accommodate the full hand. Without doubt cork is the best material; the new rubber grips should be avoided on a flyrod as they are only suitable where casting is infrequent.

Rod rings are very important, and here the angler is offered a bewildering choice. Some of the new designs are very good, but many are the result of manufacturing developments that suit the makers rather than the angler. The old-style snake rings are hard to beat – they do not impair the casting action of the rod or impede the passage of the line, they are hard wearing and very seldom damaged. It is the butt-ring and the end-ring where special attention is required, as they receive 90 per cent of the wear. For many years it was the custom to line these rings with agate, now a thing of the past, but imitation agate (plastic or glass) should be avoided as it is a very poor substitute. Metallic alloy, especially hardened, is vastly superior.

The reel is not an important item of flyfishing tackle; to most flyfishermen it is just a useful item on which to store the portion of line not in use. To a certain extent this is correct thinking, but the reel does have other aspects and cannot be so lightly dismissed. Reels do not – or should not – have the function of balancing the rod; a top-heavy rod can never be corrected by the addition of a heavy reel, and the reverse is just as true. A good rod should have a good balance built-in, and the reel selected should enhance that balance by not impairing the rod action in any way.

The main reason for purchasing a good quality reel should be to obtain mechanical reliability that will ensure trouble-free service over a long period. It is a waste of good money to pay for 'gimmicky' features. Look for lightness of weight, sound mechanical engineering, a good drag or check, rim control, a spool of 'open-cage' construction, and no side-play of the spool on the spindle.

The size of the reel is largely governed by the line it is intended to hold. Ideally, the smallest reel that will take your line plus 45.7 m (50 yds) of fine backing, should be your choice for river fishing. However, bear in mind that if economies have to be made when buying tackle, the reel is the place to start. Never try to save money on a rod so that a more expensive reel can be purchased. Concentrate first on your rod and line, then buy the best reel the budget will allow.

Flylines are available in a wide variety of weights, shapes and functions. The list is a long one. Many of these lines are for specialist use only; many are designed for the reservoir angler who has special needs; others are designed to catch anglers rather than fish. A wide range of colours is also available, since many anglers hold very firm views on this subject.

Basically speaking, river fishing calls for a double-taper line, not more than AFTM No. 7 in weight (preferably No. 5 or 6), and by far the most practical would be a floating line. Such a line would be designated DT5F or DT6F. The double taper has two functions; it enables the line to be turned end for end, and its long centre section of level line aids short-range casting and presentation of the fly. Most anglers think of the two ends as giving them two flylines for the price of one. This is good thinking, because that is exactly what one gets, but the line should not only be turned when one end is worn out. Like the tyres on a car, the two ends should be rotated fairly frequently to even out the wear. We still obtain double wear, but the line is less inclined to set into tight coils on the drum of the reel.

The question of colour for a flyline is a vexing one, and widely diverse views are held. It has been claimed that light-coloured lines scare fish as they pass to and fro through the air, but the advocates of these lines claim that all lines are seen by the fish in silhouette, and consequently appear black. There is truth on both sides, so let us examine the question in detail.

First, it must be said that a flyline should *never* pass to and fro over a fish, *nor* should it float over a fish where it will be seen in silhouette. Consequently, a side view of a floating line is all a fish should ever see, and this view should be kept to an absolute minimum – that is why we use a lengthy leader with a fine tippet. When a side view of the line is seen, the colour – any colour – is also seen.

So does it really matter what colour a flyline is? Yes, it does. It is most important for the angler that he should be able to see his line on the surface clearly; direction is all-important when fishing the dry fly, and when fishing the wet fly possible 'takes' can often be detected by watching the tip of the line. Some anglers' eyesight is better than others, and they will claim that they can see a dark line quite easily. But to what advantage? The line should not be seen by the fish anyway! I fish several times a week and have used a fluorescent coloured line for years – and not one adverse result has ever been noted.

The quality of a flyline *is* important, and while it is true that, in the main, 'you get what you pay for', it does not necessarily follow that the most expensive lines are the best. Some manufacturers' first-quality lines are less expensive than those of the same grade made by others, yet under normal fishing conditions little difference can be detected. Provided a 'name brand' line is purchased, in the best grade that can be afforded, it will give good service and be completely satisfactory. Look for a supple line, one with a smooth surface free of bumps and a lack of tendency to set in hard coils. The secret is to maintain the line in top condition by frequent washing in soapy water, drying off with a paper towel, then lightly applying a good line cleaner that contains a lubricant. Grease should never be used as it causes the surface coating of the line to degenerate.

Tapered leaders can be purchased ready made up, either knotted to form the taper or in a continuous tapered length.

New-style braided tapered leaders are also now on the market. Knotted leaders are always difficult to straighten out, especially in the region of the knots, whereas the continuous-tapered type straighten quite easily when rubbed with a piece of india rubber. The braided leader requires no treatment at all as it is completely supple under all conditions.

All the above leaders will be found satisfactory in use, but experience has shown that the braided leader has advantages the others do not possess. The suppleness of this type of leader is a considerable aid to casting, the thicker butt end gives a very smooth turnover of the line, resulting in a better presentation of the fly, and it is less expensive in use as tippets are easily changed without upsetting the 'balance' of the leader.

A lot of nonsense is often written about leader lengths. A leader should be as long as possible without becoming impracticable to cast. Very few anglers have the ability to cast a leader that is much longer than the rod they are using, consequently, a leader of 2.7 m (9 ft) is a good practical length, and should suffice for all our needs when river fishing.

We will discuss flies at a later stage, but while on the subject of tackle we must mention the fly box. All tackle shops offer a wide choice of boxes – but how very difficult to find the perfect one! Wet flies are not a problem, but dry flies are a totally different matter. It is the pristine condition of a dry fly that contributes so much to the results obtained; a crushed dry fly is a useless item. Nowhere near enough attention is paid to this point. The fly is probably the cheapest part of the equipment – but it is the item which actually takes the fish. The only practical way to carry these flies is in a box that has separate compartments. Provided the compartments are large enough, several flies can be placed in each without getting crushed, and the lid of such a box can be lined with a material into which the wet flies can be anchored. Choose your fly box with care.

Before we discuss accessories in general, let us briefly mention the landing net. This is an important item of tackle, ignored for most of the time except when needed; then its smooth function becomes of paramount importance. Later on we will discuss the net and its use in detail; for the moment it is sufficient to say that, for the mobile river flyfisherman, the best type is the collapsible net with an extending handle. The type with sidearms that swing out to form a triangular net is vastly superior to the round hoop variety. Make sure it has a good, easily released clip so that it can be slung from the belt or bag.

Almost every tackle shop is an emporium of accessories for the 'complete angler', and over a period of years we all buy many of these tempting items – it's a game that all anglers play. However, some accessories are really useful and should be looked at here.

The fishing waistcoat or vest is a boon to the flyfisherman. It enables the angler to be completely mobile, its numerous pockets hold the many small items so essential to the flyfisherman and everything is to hand without the necessity of delving into a fishing bag. It will even hold the rod while you are changing flies or dealing with a landed fish, and the landing net can be slung from one of the loops. Usually there is a large back pocket for carrying fish or a rain jacket. Some fishing waistcoats are also made to double as a life-jacket, perhaps more useful to the boat angler, but also reassuring when wading in the vicinity of deep water. This garment is a very useful item indeed.

Polarised sun-glasses are not just a useful extra, they are essential to the flyfisherman. Fishing with a fly is a visual activity that entails continuously looking at water; the reflection of light is hard on the eyes, so protection is necessary. Polarised glasses will also enable you to see the river bed clearly when wading, or searching out fish. Last, but not least, flycasting should never take place without the angler wearing eye protection.

Waders are extremely useful when fishing for trout, and a thigh-length pair can be turned down when walking along muddy banks. In most cases, a pair of gum-boots are sufficient when flyfishing for coarse fish, but a pair of waders will serve both purposes. The soles of waders always present a problem – cleated rubber soles are fine on mud, but near to useless when wading on gravel or stones. Steel-studded soles are no better on slippery stones and are, in fact, downright dangerous on any smooth surface. For many years I have used impact adhesive to glue sheet felt to the soles of my waders, leaving the studded or cleated heels for added grip. The ideal material for this used to be the hard white felt used by piano manufacturers, but this is now very difficult to obtain. The thick yellow felt (approximately 13mm/½ in thick) that is used by saddle makers is a good substitute, and can be obtained from most saddlers.

The fishing bag, or creel, is a matter of personal choice. If fish are to be retained, the creel is by far the best, as it keeps the fish in such splendid condition. Some bags have a rubberised interior for holding fish, but this is not a very good idea. True, it is easy to keep clean, but the fish do not keep in good condition. When using such a bag, wrap the fish in wet newspaper before putting them in the rubberised compartment.

Finally, the flyfisherman will require a bottle of fly floatant, a pair of nail-clippers for cutting nylon, a small stone for sharpening hooks, and a small tub of fly sinkant. The latter item may be purchased or made up at home – use fuller's earth mixed to a paste with washing-up liquid. All these items, together with the fly box, are best kept out of the fishing bag or they will get jumbled together. Store them in separate pockets where they will be easily and quickly to hand.

One last piece of advice; *never* go flyfishing without first making sure you have a fine, sharp needle in the edge of a lapel – it will prove invaluable!

# Chapter 3

# *Casting a Fly*

It is firmly believed that no written instructions, no matter how detailed, are able to teach a complete novice to cast well. This does not mean that casting cannot be improved from the written word – it most certainly can, but the results with a complete novice leave a lot to be desired. Bad habits are picked up right from the start, and no matter what quality of casting instruction is later received, somehow the bad habits always tend to return.

It is hoped that the reader already has a basic idea of casting, and is looking to improve his prowess. If this is not the case, it is strongly recommended that personal instruction be obtained. Lessons from a qualified instructor are by far the best, but most of us know a fellow angler who casts reasonably well and might be willing to give a couple of hours of instruction. A couple of hours will not teach a novice to cast expertly, but having someone available to watch progress and point out where things are going wrong will set the novice off on the right path. The instruction given in these pages is designed to assist the angler who already has some basic technique and wishes to 'iron out the wrinkles'.

There are two types of casting generally employed: the separate motion cast and the continuous motion cast. The separate motion cast, that is, what may be loosely described as the normal forward and backward cast, is the most commonly used and includes the steeple cast and various casts made to throw a curved line. The continuous motion cast describes the roll cast, the change of direction cast, and the roll cast pick-up and back cast combination.

It all sounds so very technical! However, do not let it become confusing, because we have to use these definitions to avoid misunderstandings. Let us consider the two types of casting.

It was stated above that the separate motion cast was the most commonly used. This is true, but it should not be so. Many anglers, having been taught casting basics – the forward and backward cast – never proceed beyond that point, and this is very wrong. The good flyfisher will use continuous motion casts for at least 60 per cent of his casting, and when fishing the wet fly this percentage will increase to possibly 90 per cent. So, we have a lot of ground (or water!) to cover if we intend to elevate our casting to a proficient level.

Before we proceed too far, we need to be very sure that the basic separate motion cast is being properly performed. Although simple in itself, this cast can be executed in the most horrible manner, resulting in a fly presentation that is almost useless. Properly performed, it is a delight to watch. The first thing to consider is the grip on the rod. This should be firm but definitely not tight, thumb uppermost and extended to lie along the cork grip, pointing along the rod. In other words, a light, comfortable grip. The wrist should be held naturally, not tense or slack. It is at this point that the confusion commences: some instructors advocate keeping a stiff wrist; others say the casting action should come from the wrist. Both schools of thought are partially right – and both are partially wrong.

The wrist must certainly come into play while casting, and it will do so naturally, but to try to cast solely with a wrist action will give very poor results. It is much better if the casting action originates at the shoulder, with the elbow hanging loosely down and not pressed into the side, both wrist and elbow being lightly flexed. No conscious effort should be made to bring muscles into play; good casting must always appear to be an effortless operation. Brute strength will not cast a good line, but firm, precise movements will.

The secret of a good forward and back cast lies in the mental picture imagined by the caster. During the casting process the angler has a mental picture of what he thinks is happening, and the casting action is much improved if his thoughts are along the following lines. When making the back cast he should believe that his line is being propelled backwards and *upwards*, and that the backward movement of his rod is being *stopped just short of the vertical.* He will pause while he imagines the line straightening out, then, *just before it is completely straight,* he will commence his forward cast. As the forward cast is made he

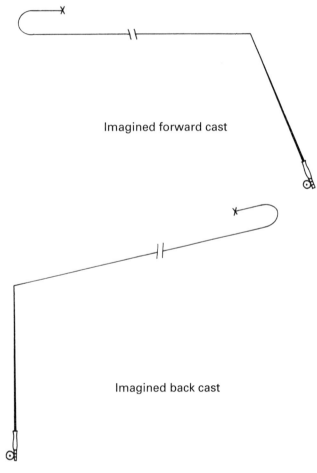

Imagined forward cast

Imagined back cast

*Fig. 1 The mental picture*
*What the caster imagines while making a standard separate motion cast.*

imagines that he is projecting the line *forward and straight out in front* (see fig. 1). All these actions are made smoothly and decisively with no brute force, but with the rod being given sufficient motion to bring its power into play.

The above description details the mental picture in the mind of the caster. What actually occurs is somewhat different! Regardless of the mental attempt to stop the rod just short of the vertical, the rod will, under its own spring and the weight of the line, continue its travel to just beyond the vertical. In

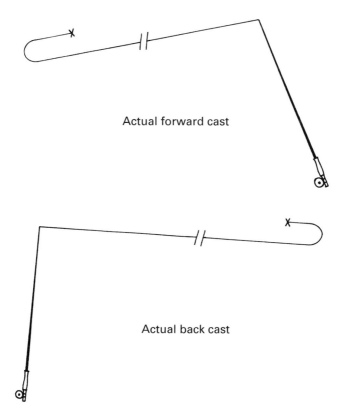

Actual forward cast

Actual back cast

*Fig. 2 The actual cast*
*What actually happens during the imagined separate motion cast.*

consequence, the line will move back in a good horizontal plane. Commencing the forward cast at that moment when the line is imagined to be *almost* straight results in a very good timing of the pause. Mentally making the forward cast directly out in front will result in the fly being 0.6–0.9 m (2–3 ft) above the water at the completion of the cast – see fig. 2. It's all in the mind!

While performing this cast, always hold the line coming from the butt ring in the left hand, so that the reel is taken out of action. Casting with the line running directly to the reel, or trapped by the hand holding the rod, gives very little control over any slack line and will spoil the cast. To enlarge on this point, for a fly to be well presented, a little slack line must be given just as the forward cast straightens out – known as 'shooting line'. This cannot be done unless the line is held in the left hand.

Shooting line is not difficult; it is a matter of timing. For the purposes of good fly presentation do not attempt to 'shoot' more than 0.6–0.9 m (2–3 ft) of line. If the required slack line is below the left hand (between the hand and the reel), there is no difficulty in letting it go at the precise moment. This additional line will enable the fly to descend to the water naturally, without any tendency to bounce back as the cast is completed (see fig. 3).

The steeple cast is a variation of this procedure that may be used when a normal back cast is obstructed. The theory is for the back cast to be projected almost vertically, then for the forward cast to be made in the normal way. This cast, it must be said, is almost pure theory and is more easily described than performed. Provided the cast is kept short – not more than 9 m (10 yd) – a reasonable steeple cast may be made, but a longer cast is beyond the capabilities of the average angler (see fig. 4).

Casting a curve in the line, so essential when fishing the dry fly to avoid drag, is a standard procedure that every angler should be able to perform. The idea is to cast a line that has a curve, or belly, upstream of the presented fly. In this manner, drag on the landed fly is delayed until the current has straightened out the line, and it is usually sufficient to give the fly a free float over the fish. There are many ways in which the curve can be accomplished, and most instructors have their own method

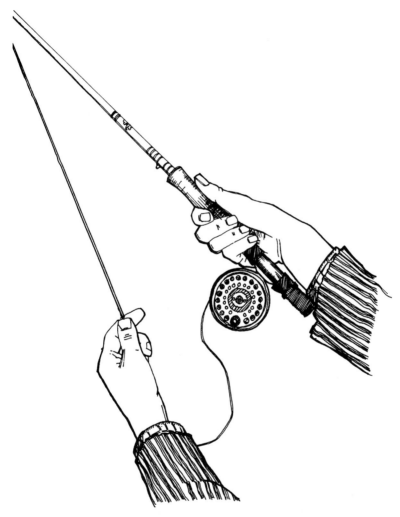

*Fig. 3 Preparation for shooting line*
*The line should always be held in this manner during all casting.*

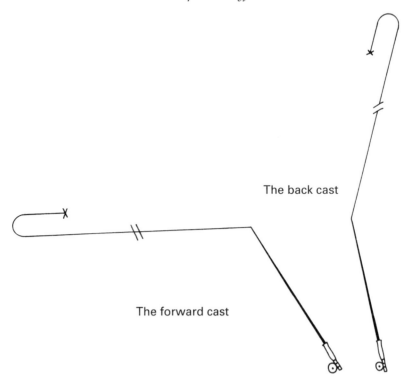

The back cast

The forward cast

*Fig. 4 The steeple cast*

of teaching it. I am no exception, and offer the following routine as one of the alternatives.

Bearing in mind that during casting the reel is directly below the rod and pointing downwards, the following procedure should be adopted. If, at the precise moment of shooting line, the hand holding the rod is twisted to the right – so that the reel is pointing to the left – the line will land on the water with a slight curve to the right. A twist in the opposite direction will make a curve to the left. Whether you curve the line to the left or the right depends on the direction of the current. Remember,

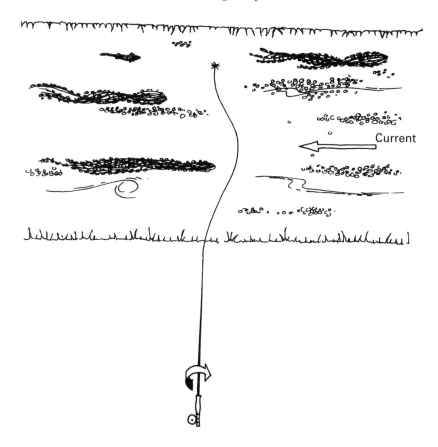

*Fig. 5 Casting a curve*
*A sharp twist of the rod to the right – so that the reel points to the left – will cast a*
*curve to the right. The twist is performed at the same time as shooting a little line.*

the objective is to place a curve or belly in the line *upstream* of the landed fly (see fig. 5).

Now let us consider the 'line entry' or, more simply, the curve in the air made by the line during its passage to and fro. Whether the line entry is broad or narrow depends to a large extent on the

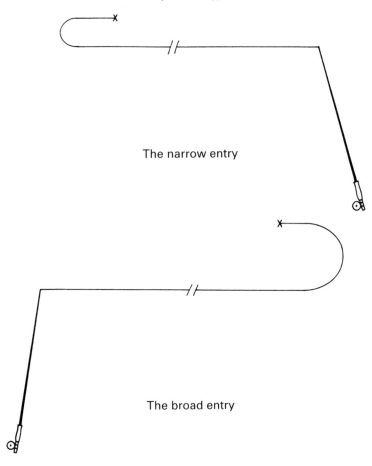

The narrow entry

The broad entry

*Fig. 6 Broad and narrow entries*

rod: a stiff rod will automatically produce a narrower entry than a whippy one. However, the actions of the angler also have a decided influence over the entry, and excessive rod movements will create a broad entry even with a stiffish rod. It is difficult to fish a dry fly well when the entry is broad; false casting to dry the fly is not so effective, and the actual presentation of the fly leaves a lot to be desired. A broad entry also hinders casting into a wind. Sometimes a broad entry is an advantage, especially when fishing a wet fly, as it prevents the fly from completely drying out between casts, and allows an immediate penetration of the water surface. The angler should pay attention to the type of line entry he produces, and practise until he can vary it at will (see fig. 6).

One final point needs to be made before we leave the subject of separate motion casts. The forward cast is a duplicate of the back cast, and any mistake in the back cast will automatically be reproduced in the forward cast. If the back cast is allowed to fall before forward motion is applied, the forward cast will also fall.

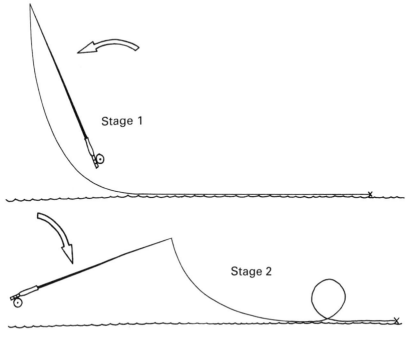

*Fig. 7 The roll cast*

Any jerky motion of the rod that produces a wavy back cast will produce a broad entry and a wavy forward cast. If you are dissatisfied with your forward cast, look to your back cast to correct matters.

Continuous motion casts enable the flyfisher to angle for fish that would otherwise be unapproachable, except, perhaps, by fishing from a different position. One of the most useful of such casts is the roll cast. We are very often in the position where obstructions behind us prevent our casting to a fish that cannot be approached from any other direction. The roll cast has the

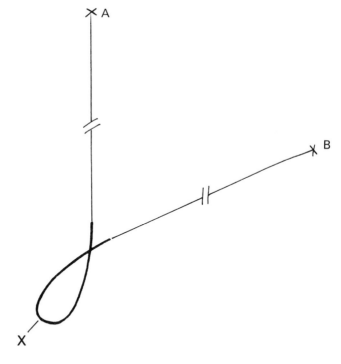

*Fig. 8 Change-of-direction cast*
*Fly at point A is re-cast to point B by making a continuous motion cast. X denotes the movement of the rod tip during the cast.*

advantage that the line never passes behind the angler from start to finish.

At the start of the roll cast the line should be extended downstream of the angler. Holding the line firmly in the left hand, raise the rod until it is a few degrees beyond the vertical, and extend your rod arm at the same time so that the reel is in the vicinity of your right ear with the rod bearing to the side at a slight angle. This will have the effect of drawing the line towards you, and is complete when the line is hanging down vertically beside you. After a very short pause the rod is then swept down sharply in the direction in which you wish to cast, and the line will be projected forward in the form of a rolling loop. This cast is not difficult to perform (see fig. 7). Practice makes perfect!

Another use of the roll cast technique is the combination roll and back cast. When fishing the wet fly, it is often necessary to use a weighted fly fished very deep, and to re-cast such a fly without bringing it to the surface first is extremely difficult, as well as very rough on the rod tip. If the roll cast is performed, the fly will be drawn to the surface gently, and at the end of the cast will actually be on the surface; it is then comparatively easy to bring the rod back into the standard back cast in the normal way.

When fishing the wet fly downstream, roll casting is almost a standard procedure, as it enables the angler to place his fly almost anywhere he wishes without having to take obstructions into consideration. An added plus is that the fly is rarely out of the water and has no opportunity to dry out.

Change-of-direction casts are not easy to perform. Many anglers obtain a change of direction by continuously false casting in the air, changing the direction a little at a time between forward and backward casts. Without doubt, this procedure works quite well when fishing the dry fly, and false casting is necessary in any case to dry the fly. In wet fly fishing it has many drawbacks, the fly is out of the water for far too long and the final presentation will be marred.

Direction can be changed by a continuous motion cast. As this cast is somewhat difficult to perform, at first attempt the line should be kept quite short, increasing length as proficiency is obtained. It is almost impossible to describe this cast in words, but a study of fig. 8 should help to make the procedure clear. The backward and forward casts are a continuous movement, with *no pause*, and it is the circular movement of the rod tip that causes the change of direction.

Casting is one of the delights of flyfishing, not just a necessary procedure, and it should be looked upon as an art form, with great pleasure to be obtained from a good performance. Good casting will not automatically catch more fish – it must be agreed that water know-how and fly presentation are more important – but if you are able to cast well it will add to the pleasure of a day out.

It is always a good idea, at the end of a fishing day, to spend 10–15 minutes at casting practice. You are already well limbered-up, the water is there, the rod in your hand – so why not? Leave the fly on – you never know!

# Chapter 4

# The Wild Trout

The roving angler, fishing various regions and localities, could be forgiven if he came to the conclusion that there were many different species of wild trout. However, this is not the case. Anglers in many localities have argued over the years, and in fact still insist, that their local trout are a separate species. The truth of the matter is that there is only one trout that is indigenous to the UK, and that is the sea, or brown trout, *Salmo trutta*. All other native trout are variants once thought to be sub-species.

We must clarify the above by saying that there are three rivers in England where rainbow trout have become acclimatised over the years and are spawning regularly. They have, in fact, become wild rainbows. This is the only known exception, as these fish are of the species *Salmo irrideus*.

It is the ability of the wild 'brownie' to vary so considerably according to the local environment that has caused this confusion. Not only does the colour vary, but the size and distribution of the spots, and, in some cases, even the bodily shape of the fish. These variations are, in the main, caused by the acidity or alkalinity of the water, and the type of food these waters contain.

Alkaline waters – those from a chalk or limestone source – are usually abundant in plant life, resulting in a prolific insect population. Trout from such waters grow well on the unlimited food supply, and the spots become enlarged – so large that sometimes they fuse together. The food is also rich in fats which produce a substance called guanine in the fish, giving the fish a decidedly silvery hue. Such fish are the 'fat cats' of the trout world.

Most trout rivers and streams of the hill or mountain areas are very acid, added to which many are spate waters. These acid waters do not encourage plant life, and although insect life is always present, it is usually in short supply. This is particularly true of the spate river, and we will discuss these waters later as their problems are distinct and separate. Trout from acid waters are, on average, smaller and more brightly coloured, with smaller and widely separated spots, and a body colour often of a golden hue.

Body colour – in fact all colour – is caused by pigmentation in the skin, which is partly influenced by the pH value of the water. To a certain extent the coloration is a camouflage, and the colour of the water and stream bed will also influence that of the fish.

Very dark fish are sometimes encountered, possibly due to the peaty nature of the water. However, these should not be confused with the almost black appearance of sick fish, which should always be killed immediately, before they spread disease to the rest of the trout population.

A wild river trout is decidedly old at seven years, and from that point on deterioration is rapid. Size depends entirely on the abundance of the available food supply, and no hard and fast indication can be given, but as a general guide, a reasonably well-fed trout of 0.3 m (12 in) should weigh about 340 g (12 oz).

The food of trout consists of flies that hatch from the water or find their way to the water, underwater larvae and insects, terrestrial insects that fall onto the water, worms and smaller fish. For an abundance of these food forms to be present, the water needs to be clean, unpolluted, and to have a stream bed of rock or gravel.

The wild brown trout is an extremely wary creature. The question is often asked whether a fish can hear sounds. The answer is that it cannot, not in the sense that we hear, but it can certainly 'hear' in a different way. Vibrations through the water, even the slightest tremors, are picked up by the nervous system along the lateral line and in the skin of the fish. Sounds such as human shouting, motor horns, music, and so on, cannot be heard unless their vibrations enter the water, but footfalls on the bank, dropped tackle, the crunch of gravel underfoot, all such sounds are picked up as vibrations.

In fishes, taste is completely absent due to a lack of taste buds, and so it is useless trying to flavour flies to make them more attractive. Many years ago there were certain oils on the market for this purpose (some may still be available), but they can do nothing for us. The sense of smell is a different matter. Trout cannot 'smell' as we are able to do using our respiratory organs, but they can certainly pick up odours. By experiment it has been found that certain odours attract, while others repel, so make sure your fingers are not tainted with any substance when handling artificial flies.

The trout gives the impression of having very keen eyesight, and this is generally believed to be so, but there are certain aspects of its vision that need closer examination. The pupil of the eye has no means to contract as a protection against light, nor has the trout any eyelids or eyelashes that can be manipulated to help obscure light. Consequently, bright light, such as sunlight, dazzles and renders objects hazy. If we fish with the sun behind us – provided no shadow falls near the fish – we provide a very hazy outline, not at all clearly seen.

The eyes also point forward and tilt upwards, making it almost impossible for the trout to see anything below or behind. We can certainly capitalise on this; provided we are behind the fish we can be assured that we are obscured from view, and in the case of the trout this is simplified as they invariably lie facing upstream. Be warned, however: the vibrations we set up during our approach will certainly warn the trout of our presence, and if we are to the side of him – closer than 9 m (10 yd) – we will certainly be seen.

What has been said about the dazzling effects of sunlight can also be turned to our advantage when casting a fly. In a dull light, such as shade or shadow, the vision of a trout is near perfect, every detail of the artificial fly will be clearly seen, but if we cast so that the fly is between the trout and the sun it is a different matter. To look at the fly the trout also has to look in the direction of the sun, so the fraudulent nature of the artificial fly is somewhat obscured.

Without doubt trout are able to differentiate between colours, and we must take this ability into account when choosing or designing an artificial fly. In the underwater world of the trout, colours are inclined to be drab – browns, olives, and greys predominate; sometimes greens and shades of purple are present. What we know as primary colours, the reds, blues and yellows, are absent. It is perhaps for this reason that the wild trout, the brownie, is seldom attracted by primary colours – these colours are just not associated with food. Sometimes primary colours are used when tying lures, but this is for a different reason; the lures are intended to represent small bait fish, and the colour is used to give the impression of sudden and rapid movement.

Silver or gold tinsel is often used when dressing a trout fly, and cannot be included in the above remarks. Tinsel is used for reflecting underwater objects, or to glint or flash in the sunlight. All these effects seem natural to the trout; they draw attention to the fly and add to its attraction.

From time to time, the river angler will come across rainbow trout, and these will invariably be stock fish that have been hatchery bred. As previously mentioned, rainbows have become acclimatised in a few waters, but the angler will be very fortunate indeed if he comes into contact with one of these. Some angling clubs, many syndicates, and also a number of private owners are now stocking their rivers with rainbows. I find no merit in this practice. The rainbow will not spawn in these waters, and the numbers stocked are in direct ratio to the number expected to be caught. The rainbow is a heavy feeder, consuming approximately twice the daily intake of the native brown, and consequently depletes the food supply available. This heavy feeding brings with it rapid growth – a rainbow will add about 0.5 kg (1 lb) in weight per year – as its weight increases so does the food requirement, all to the detriment of the native browns.

Could the reason for stocking rainbows be that they are easier to catch? It has been said many times that an ex-hatchery fish quickly reverts to nature once it is put in open water, but do not forget – rainbows are always easier to catch than wild brownies. If fishing pressure dictates that stocking is necessary, why not stock with hatchery browns?

Notwithstanding the above comments, the rainbow trout is a beautiful fish and affords good sport for the flyfisherman. Its natural habitat is the western seaboard of the North American continent where there are two distinct species; the sea-going steelhead and the non-migratory rainbow. They were introduced into the UK in the 1880s, and the two species have been indiscriminately interbred in the hatcheries, the result being the cross-bred fish now common in the UK, known as *Salmo irrideus*.

There are distinct differences between rainbows and browns that need to be remembered when fishing for them, and perhaps the most obvious is the greed for food. The food requirements of the rainbow make it a far less wary fish, and certainly less selective in its feeding habits. True, it can be very selective at times, especially when a heavy hatch is in progress, but even then it can sometimes be tempted by a bright lure. The rainbow will willingly take all the usual drab flies associated with the brown, but in addition will often be tempted by gaily coloured flies in primary colours that the brown will ignore.

The fight put up by these two trout species is also very different: whereas the brown is a dogged fighter, an expert at using snags to obtain its freedom, the rainbow is flamboyant by comparison. A hooked rainbow will invariably make several jumps, sometimes one after another, which will be hard but with no real attempt to head for snags; it rarely dives for cover and doggedly refuses to be moved. An exciting fish!

Both the brown and the rainbow are excellent fare for the table, and both fish will keep better after capture if they are immediately gutted. As a golden rule, never re-wash the fish with water during the day after it has been gutted and creeled, as this spoils the flesh for the kitchen.

It is, perhaps, the culinary delights of these fish that are the biggest drawback to their conservation. In my view, official bag limits are too high, and it is up to all of us to impose our own limits. By all means have the occasional trout for the table, but *please* do not kill just for the sake of taking them home to show you have had a good day. Everyone should try to leave a few for next time.

# Chapter 5

# *Locating Trout*

Locating suitable waters for trout fishing is considerably easier than locating the fish themselves. If you are visiting a new area and are a total stranger, the local tackle shop is usually a mine of information, and quite a number are agents for the local fishing clubs and sell daily or weekly tickets. It is also worth visiting or writing to the area tourist board, some of which have brochures giving full details of sporting activities available. Then there are regional water authorities, many of whom publish illustrated booklets on fishing in their area.

Although obtaining information is easy, many a day's fishing has been spoilt by not being able to find the exact location of the fishing rights. Information on club tickets and in brochures is rarely adequate, and it is quite common for access points to the water to be most obscure. Nothing is more irritating than to spend half your valuable day knocking on farmhouse doors for information – a waste of good fishing time! It is well worth while to purchase an Ordnance Survey map of any area you intend to fish, then to ask the local tackle shop to pinpoint the exact location and the access points. Once the water has been located, comes the difficult part – locating the fish. Every water is different, and to be successful you must be able to 'read' the water to decide confidently on the tactics necessary.

The requirements of trout are really twofold: they must have food, and they need to pursue that food in comparative safety. The current of a river acts somewhat like a conveyor belt, carrying a constant supply of food particles downstream, and the trout do not have to move very much to forage for sustenance. Trout take up feeding stations where the current will do the job for them, and these feeding stations or lies are selected with an eye for safety. To a trout safety is usually measured in terms of cover, either overhead or nearby underwater, and the best locations are always taken up by the largest fish.

To 'read' water well, you must be able to recognise a good trout lie, one that not only offers safety, but is also well served by the current for the supply of food. This does not mean that a good lie needs to be in the main stream; on the contrary, a trout will want to maintain its feeding station with the minimum of effort. There is no point in expending more energy to obtain the food than the food will replace. Fig. 9 shows two examples of rock cover that meet these requirements.

Submerged rock

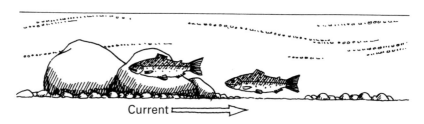

Current

Protruding rock

Current

*Fig. 9 Rock cover*
*Both submerged and protruding rocks provide feeding stations for trout. In the case of the submerged rock, food can pass overhead, and a dry fly is effective. Wet flies must be used to fish round the protruding rock.*

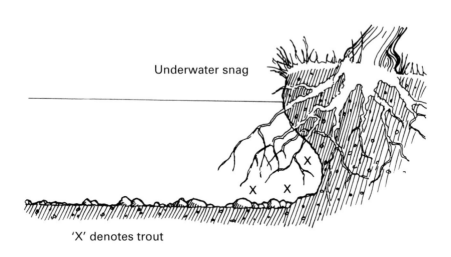

Underwater snag

'X' denotes trout

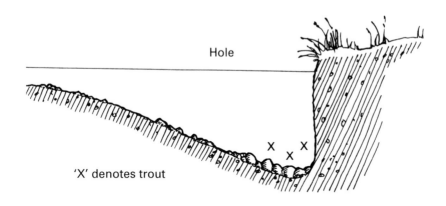

Hole

'X' denotes trout

*Fig. 10 Favourite trout lies*
*Both of the above are favourite trout lies. Trout among snags will take food passing*
*by, but care is needed to prevent them returning to the snags after hooking. Trout*
*deep in a hole will rarely rise to a fly; wet flies fished deep are the most effective.*

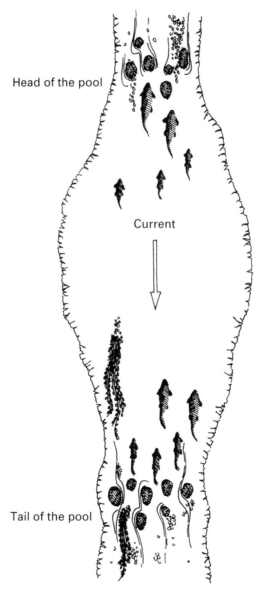

Head of the pool

Current

Tail of the pool

*Fig. 11 The pool*
*Trout will lie at both the head and tail of a pool, with the largest out in front for the*
*first choice of food brought by the current.*

The submerged rock provides cover, and also a lie that is out of the main current so that little energy is required for the fish to maintain its station, while food particles are carried overhead as well as to both sides of the rock. The rock does not have to be large to meet these requirements; a good-sized stone will serve for a medium-size trout. These submerged rock lies are not too difficult to locate – they always cause a measure of turbulence on the water surface that appears slightly downstream of the rock itself.

The protruding rock, while providing cover and an easy station to maintain, has the disadvantage that no food is able to pass overhead. Sometimes trout will take up a lie in front of such a rock – there is always a small pocket of slack water in front where the current divides, and the frontal lie gives full access to all food, including that which is overhead – but most trout will be found behind the rock.

Undercut banks, especially those where tree roots enter the water (see fig. 10), are another favourite lie. Underwater as well as overhead cover is provided, and nothing interrupts the flow of food. Sometimes the undercutting of a bank results in a deep hole in the stream bed, and trout will congregate in the depression created. Little cover is available, but the depth of the water gives an element of safety and, of course, food is inclined to accumulate in the hollow (see fig. 10).

Pools are always likely places for trout, and during the day the fish tend to congregate at either the head of the pool or the tail, particularly if there are rock formations. If no rock formations are present, then expect to find the trout in the deepest portion of the pool (see fig. 11). A series of rocks at the head of a pool may be fished almost individually, treating each one as a separate piece of cover, but at the tail of the pool much more caution is necessary. Fish at the tail end usually have smooth water ahead of them and therefore a much better view of what is happening. Often the tail of a pool is better fished from below the pool itself, with the angler keeping as low as possible to hide his movements. When trout are suspected of being in the depths of a pool, a weighted wet fly technique, will bring the best results.

When visiting unfamiliar water for the first time, the angler should not be in any hurry to start fishing. Look the water over very carefully and make a mental note of all likely lies; sometimes a rise will be seen and the lie can be noted for future attention. At this stage of the day's fishing great care is needed not to disturb the water. It is only too easy to ruin your prospects by heavy footfalls along the bank, or by making yourself too visible to the fish. If you intend to wade, decide on the best points to enter the water, places that will not disturb areas you intend to fish later. The position of the sun should also be carefully noted so that full advantage can be taken of light and shadow. Always concentrate on a reasonably short stretch of water, and determine to fish that stretch to its maximum potential, for there is little point in moving on to new water when the water in front of you has not been fished-out. Most rivers that support a wild trout population have several hundred trout to the mile; bear this point in mind and persevere until you locate them. Move on only when a disturbance of some kind – perhaps the taking of a fish – renders any further fishing in that place out of the question.

Sometimes a local angler is met on the water, and advice is freely given, but this type of information is usually based on where fish have been caught in the past, perhaps long ago. Whenever possible, it is better to rely on your own prowess in 'reading' water – the reason why it is so important to become efficient in this respect. There is one source of local information that is usually very reliable – local small boys can nearly always tell you where the deep holes are, and their assessment of the depth is surprisingly accurate. But make very sure that the reason for your approach is made obvious from the start.

As a last piece of advice on locating trout, it might be a good idea to mention the Jones brothers, who lived in a heavily industrialised area. Their local river could only be classed as a third-rate trout water, and that description is on the generous side. The river was very heavily fished by the locals, and all methods were used to extract trout – bait fishing, spinning, flyfishing – none of which was particularly successful. It was a good day that resulted in the occasional trout being taken. The Jones brothers fished on a regular basis, always using a fly, and their results were very different, each of the brothers taking their limit regularly. One day, in the local, someone asked the brothers the secret of their success. The elder Jones thought carefully for a moment, then he said: 'Perhaps it's because we always fish where the other chaps don't bother; they say that there are no fish there, but we find them!'

*Chapter 6*

# Coarse Fish –
# The Free-Risers

Although, as previously mentioned, many species of coarse fish will take the odd insect as part of their daily diet, a few are confirmed in this habit, and will willingly take an artificial. For the sake of clarity we will designate these as the 'free-risers', in contrast to the predatory species that will be considered later.

## Chub

The chub is widely distributed in the UK, and is a very worth-while quarry for the flyfisherman. In various localities nicknames such as 'chevin', 'loggerhead' and 'alderman', were once frequently encountered. This is a bulky fish that grows to a good size, and specimens of 0.9–1.4 kg (2–3 lb) are commonly taken on a fly.

Chub are easily located if their requirements are very carefully considered. Water depths of between 0.9–1.5 m (3–5 ft) are preferred, particularly if the river bed is sand or gravel. They invariably lie in slack water, but always close to a good current. The most necessary of their requirements is shady cover, and overhanging alders are a firm favourite – hence the nickname 'alderman' (see fig. 12).

The eyesight of chub is extremely keen, and in their shady lies very little escapes their attention. Without doubt, this fish is the most sensitive of all the coarse species to underwater vibrations, and the utmost care is needed in approaching it. It would be wrong to think of a chub as a particularly wary fish;

just one that is always fully aware of its surroundings.

When angling for chub with a fly, the main problem is the difficulty of casting to them due to the inaccessible lies they choose. To overcome this problem, it is often advisable to fish downstream to them, even with a dry fly; with care it can be

'X' denotes chub

*Fig. 12 Chub lies*

floated downstream with very little drag, but one must pay out line very carefully. In any case, drag is not as important with chub as it is with trout. Sometimes the very action of a dragged fly seems to be an added attraction to a feeding, active chub.

When fishing for chub avoid the use of very fine tippets; these fish are heavy fighters and cause quite a commotion when hooked, and the first plunge of a good-sized chub will break any tippet finer than 3x. It is impossible to avoid their initial plunge, and the disturbance created makes it a waste of time to continue fishing the same swim, so after taking a large chub move off along the river to seek another.

Flies for chub need to be very 'buggy' in appearance, and a good mouthful, so flies tied on size 10 long-shank hooks are about right. Several chub patterns will be described in detail later, when we consider flies in general. Although flies may be fished wet or dry, and both are productive, a semi-sunken dry fly is perhaps the best, especially if it is 'buggy' and fished with a slight drag. One last tip: a chub is a heavy fish in the water and is inclined to explode into violent action when hooked, so take care not to be heavy-handed when striking. Just tighten the line and allow the fish to hook itself.

## Dace

The dace also enjoys a wide distribution and is a delightful fish to take on a fly. I have a soft spot for this fish, as a dace was the very first fish I ever took on a fly – and it was a good one, just under 340 g (12 oz)! Dace of over 0.45 kg (1 lb) are very rare, and should not be expected; the average size is about 230 g (8 oz).

Dace prefer shallow, fast water, and the cleaner the better. In fact, it is surprising how strong a current they will tolerate. My first dace took a dry fly that was almost drowned in the white water at the tail of a weir.

It is easy to confuse the dace with a small chub, but a careful examination will show that the fins of a dace are quite pale when compared with those of a chub; also the dorsal and anal fins of a

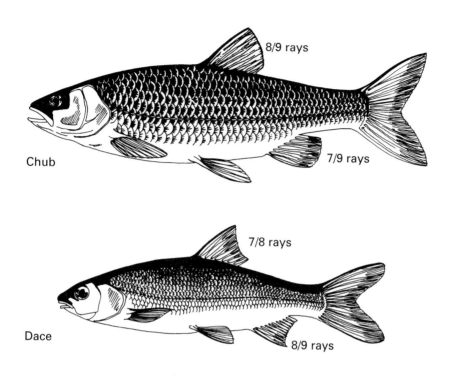

8/9 rays

Chub

7/9 rays

7/8 rays

Dace

8/9 rays

*Fig. 13 Some external differences between chub and dace*

dace are concave, whereas those of a chub are decidedly convex (see fig. 13).

Very large shoals of dace may be encountered, and a hooked, struggling fish can very easily frighten the shoal. Always try to draw a hooked fish away from the shoal quickly with the minimum splashing on the surface; with care several fish can be caught from the shoal before the rest become frightened and disperse. Summer evenings on the River Ouse, when the dace seemed to be rising from bank to bank come to mind. With two companions, I have often taken 20 or more fish from the same shoal, all without moving our position.

Dace will take flies fished both wet or dry, but the dry fly is by far the most productive. Almost any fly pattern will do, but over the years experience has shown that a black fly is usually preferred. A black gnat or coachman are both ideal. One very important point is the size of the fly, the best results being obtained from flies smaller than size 16.

Although dace will put up a good fight for their size, a 5x or 6x tippet is quite satisfactory under normal conditions. They are fast, splashy risers, and the strike needs to be very rapid. If you need practice to sharpen-up your reaction time – try flyfishing for dace!

## Golden rudd

The rudd is not truly a river fish as it inhabits areas of still water, but nevertheless, many lakes and ponds are fed by rivers and streams, and the roving angler may have the opportunity to fish for them. The rudd is not widely distributed, and you will be fortunate to find an area where they are plentiful. They are beautiful fish – magnificent would be a better description – with a green/brown back, golden sides, and vivid scarlet ventral fins. The size varies, depending on the environment, but fish up to 1.1 kg (2½ lb) can be expected on a fly.

Rudd prefer still water, and are often found in completely weed-choked areas. The weeds do not seem to bother them, and they move quite freely in large shoals through the tangle. The shoals are of mixed size, and can often be located by throwing one or two small pieces of bread onto the water surface, or sometimes a series of rises will indicate the position of a passing shoal.

The rudd is a very free-rising fish, but one with decided peculiarities that need to be constantly borne in mind. Wet fly fishing is normally impossible, due to the dense weed, so we will concentrate on the dry fly aspects.

Although the species will eagerly take bait that is presented on quite large hooks (size 6 is not unusual), any fly larger than size 18 is usually completely ignored. The fly pattern does not seem to be important; even when a hatch of olive flies is taking place the rudd will still take a completely different pattern. I have found them to be totally unselective. In fact, under most conditions a Royal Coachman has proved to be a favourite fly.

Another peculiarity of rudd is that they rarely take flies that move. After carefully observing their approach over a number of years, my conclusion is that they much prefer dead insects caught in the surface film. An instance comes to mind when a fly was unintentionally slightly twitched after being cast; a large rudd nosed up to the fly, then proceeded to push the fly along the surface for at least 0.6 m (2 ft) before deciding to take it. It can only be assumed that this was to 'ensure' it was lifeless.

The procedure when fishing for rudd is first to locate a shoal, then to cast to the centre of the rises, leaving the fly completely

*A 2¼ lb golden rudd taken on a Royal Coachman*

stationary. The takes are rarely splashy, a sudden sip and the fly has gone. The rudd will eject an artificial fly so quickly that striking is almost always too late, so try to cast a very straight line so that the fish is self-hooked. Rudd are not strong-fighting fish – they usually dive into the choked weeds and sullenly resist being moved, but such weeds are rarely that thick and a steady pressure should overcome the difficulty. With patience, a well-hooked rudd seldom gets away.

The size of the shoals is sometimes quite immense. On many a summer evening I and my companions, fishing almost side by side, have taken more than 40 rudd within two hours. Whenever the opportunity presents itself, never neglect to fish for this peculiar, but very beautiful, species.

Before we leave the subject of 'free-risers', it should be mentioned that great care is necessary when returning them to the water. Just because they are termed 'coarse' fish does not mean they are hardy; damage can easily be inflicted by rough handling. A gently handled fish will survive the trauma of being caught – but one roughly thrown back will probably die, or even spread disease throughout the whole shoal.

*Chapter 7*

# *Coarse Fish –*
# *The Predators*

Predatory fish are not usually associated with flyfishing, perhaps because flies do not normally figure in their diet, but they can certainly be caught on fly tackle. Their normal diet of small fish can be simulated with fly lures, easily cast by a flyrod. The resulting sport on this kind of tackle can only be described as outstanding.

## Perch

The perch is a common fish; it breeds prolifically, to the point of being a nuisance in many waters. With a wide distribution, it may be found in ponds, lakes, canals, reservoirs, rivers and streams. Perch are gregarious, some of the shoals being very large and always containing fish of mixed sizes. They have a possible life-span of about five years and can grow to a weight of about 2 kg (4½ lb). Once perch are over 1.4 kg (3 lb), they become very solitary and leave shoals. More probably, the shoals avoid them, for perch have no hesitation in eating their own kind.

When flyfishing for perch it is annoying to have the fly constantly taken by small ones, but there is nothing one can do about it as even a large lure will still be attacked. Perseverance will pay off, however, for the shoals often contain many fish of over 340 g (12 oz) that will give excellent sport.

Perch shoals congregate in slack water, especially in the vicinity of rushes. Their coloration indicates their natural habitat – the green/brown/golden body complete with dark bars is perfectly camouflaged among the vegetation. For some reason, perch also remain in the vicinity of sunken wooden piles; small wooden bridges or landing stages always seem to have a resident perch community nearby. When resting, they will congregate in the deepest holes available or among rushes and underwater plant life (see fig. 14).

Although bright wet flies will take perch, it is always better to fish with a lure which may attract the larger fish. When we discuss flies and lures in detail, several good perch patterns will be mentioned. Lures should be tied on size 8 or 10 long-shank hooks, and tinsel is a necessary ingredient of the dressing. Bright colours always attract, and reds and yellows may be incorporated in all lures.

The writer has experimented with black and white lures, and results have been promising. Under very overcast conditions the

*A nice perch taken on a Mini-Lure*

'X' denotes perch

*Fig. 14 Perch lies*
*Perch shoals always congregate in semi-slack water in the vicinity of rushes,*
*underwater plants and sunken wood piles.*

Black Ghost lure seems to be particularly attractive to the larger fish.

|  | *Black Ghost* |
| --- | --- |
| Body: | Black silk – dressed fat |
| Ribbing: | Silver tinsel |
| Wing: | White hair |
| Tail: | Yellow hackle fibres |
| Throat: | Yellow hackle fibres |

All lures, as well as wet flies, should have the tail dressed very short indeed. Perch invariably strike at their prey from the rear, and seem to miss as many times as they hit. Because of this, the angler will feel many sharp plucks at the fly as it is retrieved. Try to ignore these attempted attacks and continue retrieving the fly with short, sharp pulls until a fish is solidly felt, then strike.

Large perch fight very well and will give excellent sport. Rarely does the fight frighten off the shoal; in fact it is quite common to see several other perch follow the captive to the net. Only very large perch are at all wary but these are extremely so – solitary fish of over 1.4 kg (3 lb) take a lot of outwitting.

Extreme care is needed when handling perch, even the small ones, for the dorsal fin has boney spines which can inflict nasty wounds that may turn septic. Hold the fish in a wet cloth to unhook it, or smooth the dorsal fin carefully down by passing the hand from the head towards the tail.

Large perch will not disgrace the table; on the contrary, they make excellent eating if they come from clean water. Any trace of muddy taste can be eliminated by using a little salt and onion in the cooking.

## Pike

Stories about giant pike are legendary; everyone has heard about enormous pike that are reputed to have attacked bathers, eaten ducks whole, attacked swimming dogs, and so on. Pike are variously described as 'ghastly brutes', 'ugly', 'vicious' and 'repulsive'. Is this truth or fancy? It all sounds good in the telling and, as they say, 'there is no smoke without fire!' On average, however, the pike is simply another fresh-water predator.

Like the perch, the pike is widely distributed, and the habitat it prefers is also similar. The coloration is again the key – the green-and-yellow mottled markings make a perfect camouflage against rushes and underwater vegetation. Unlike the perch, the pike is a solitary fish from a very early age. Size is almost impossible to determine; it is a matter of record that pike can grow to over 31.7 kg (70 lb) – such fish would be approximately 1.5 m (5 ft) long, but this is far from normal. Any pike over 4.5 kg (10 lb) is almost certainly female. The pike has a long life span, 30 years has been recorded, and in large open waters, such as the Irish loughs, the final size can only be a matter for conjecture. The inland river fish is a totally different matter, and in these pages we are concerned with taking the smaller river 'jack' – between 1.8–3.6 kg (4–8 lb) – on a flyrod.

Before we discuss angling for this fish we need to know a good deal more about its physical attributes and habits. The pike is a very spasmodic feeder. At times the feeding is voracious, and attacks are made on any living thing, of suitable size, that comes into view, but at other times the pike will lie completely dormant and cannot be tempted by anything. Sometimes shoals of small fish will swim unconcerned close to a pike's snout; obviously, a non-feeding pike is no danger to them. So if your angling is unsuccessful on a particular day, it is not necessarily your tactics which are at fault. Pike may be caught throughout the coarse fishing season, but the end of September onwards will produce the best results. During the summer months angling for pike should take place between sunrise and 10–11 a.m.

The mouth of a pike is large and very bony, and the easiest way to describe the teeth is to say that the mouth fairly bristles with them. Apart from the fixed teeth, the pike has vomer teeth on the roof of the mouth (the palate). These backward-facing teeth allow prey to pass down the gullet only; in fact, a pike has the utmost difficulty in ejecting any unwanted item. Due to the bony structure of the mouth very little damage is done by hooking a pike (although some damage is unavoidable); and very seldom do pike suffer many ill effects from the experience.

The utmost care must be taken when removing hooks from the

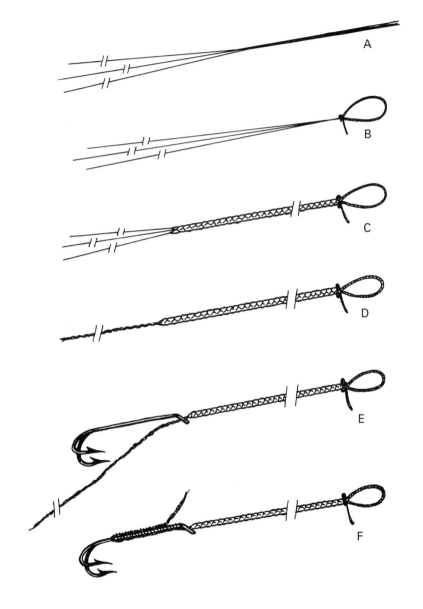

*Fig. 15 Pike fly trace*

mouth or a nasty wound may be the result. One of those gadgets called a 'pike gag' may be used to hold the mouth open while the hooks are removed with the help of a pair of small-nosed pliers, but this can damage the mouth of a pike.

All these teeth create a real problem for the pike flyfisherman, as the average nylon fly leader is absolutely useless. This problem can be overcome by using a special fly trace (see fig. 15).

The construction is quite easy. (a) Three strands of 2x nylon, 0.55 m (1½ ft) long, are glued together at one end, using any type of paper glue – golden gum is ideal. While the end is still tacky (b) a loop is tied using a standard nylon knot. After the loop is tied the gum is washed off in warm water. The three strands are then close-plaited (c) for a length of 203 mm (8 in), and the free ends are glued together (d), again with golden gum. The gummed end is passed through the eye of the hook (e) and bound down as shown in (f) – normal tying silk can be used for this purpose. After trimming all the loose ends, the job is complete.

Obviously, this trace is a long way from being ideal, and it will suffer damage from the pike's teeth over a period of time, but it is surprising how resilient a close plait of nylon can be. When fishing, the trace can be directly attached to the end of a 1.5 m (5 ft) level leader of nylon which has a breaking strain of 8 kg (18 lb).

Hooks may be doubles or trebles. A large salmon double with a long shank is quite suitable, but it is now possible to obtain trebles with extended shanks, intended for tube flies, and the angler may prefer these.

The lure itself should be 76–114 mm (3–3½ in) long, tied so that the hooks are centrally located. A simple pattern is shown in fig. 16 and, although colours may be varied it would be wise to keep to the general pattern. In flyfishing, experience shows that a pike will not take a stationary prey, but is always interested if the prey appears to be in difficulties. If the lure is allowed to sink before it is retrieved in short rapid jerks, the materials will give motion to it. The marabou will pulsate with short sharp jerks, the fine hair will undulate, and the golden pheasant tippet-head will simulate open gills – the rest is up to the pike!

Fish the lure along rushes, or close to weed beds, and try to work the lure at a level between 76–460 mm (3–18 in) off the bottom. When the lure is hit, strike hard by lowering the rod to water level and striking sideways. It does no harm to strike several times, but never strike in an upward direction. A hooked pike will try to thresh on the surface with mouth open to eject the lure, so you must overcome this with side-strain applied very low – if necessary put your rod tip in the water. Pike up to 3.5 kg (8 lb) may be safely netted – a gaff is not necessary – but

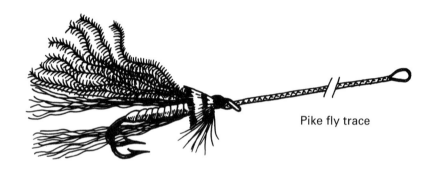

Pike fly trace

DRESSING

| Hook | : Large salmon double |
| Body | : Tinsel |
| Over-wing | : Marabou plumes – white |
| Top Wing | : Black hair |
| Bottom Wing | : White hair |
| Head | : Golden pheasant tippet |
| Throat | : Red hackle fibres |

*Fig. 16 Pike fly*
*The dressing may be varied. Marabou plumes may be yellow; bottom and upper wings may be brown and yellow. The head and throat should be as shown.*

try to net tail-first to keep its teeth from snagging the mesh of the net.

The pike makes excellent eating if taken from clean water. I have good memories of camping holidays when the evening meal very often consisted of pike cutlets fried in golden butter – delicious!

## Chapter 8

# Occasional Encounters

It is perhaps true to say that nearly all coarse fish will, from time to time, consume insects, grubs and crustaceans as part of their daily diet. Even the confirmed bottom-feeders are not averse to eating the minute animal life they disturb in their constant foraging into the detritus and mulm that often carpets their habitat.

Surprisingly often our fly presentation in pursuit of a specific quarry results in an unexpected encounter. Two species that are prime candidates come to mind: the various varieties of bream and carp.

The bream is a common fish, widely distributed. It has a heavy, deep-bodied appearance – perhaps slab-sided would be a more apt description. It is usually a browny bronze colour, but can vary enormously depending on the habitat; at times it is almost golden olive. Bream have been known to weigh up to 5.5 kg (12 lb plus), but such large fish are extremely rare. However, fish of 1–2 kg (2½–5 lb) are quite common, and can provide good sport for the flyfisher.

Their normal habitat is slow-flowing or still water, such as lakes, reservoirs and canals. Feeding takes place almost exclusively on the bottom by blowing away mud etc. to find insect larvae or small crustaceans. However, at times bream will feed in mid-water, but will almost never rise to surface food. When feeding in mid-water they have been known to chase and consume small fish fry.

Bream are rarely the intended quarry of the flyfisher, but from time to time are taken on weighted wet flies and nymphs fished very close to the bottom. Small lures (fish fry simulators) fished

*Working terrestrial flies at very close quarters under overhanging branches.*

*There has to be chub under those trees!*

*A good selection of terrestrial flies for the summer months.*

*1. Picket Finn   2. Beetle   3. Woolly Worm   4. Bumble   5. Mini-Lure   6. Red Ant*
*7. Catbug   8. Green Caterpillar   9. Thief*

in mid-water for perch have also been known to take bream occasionally.

The fight to land a good-sized bream can be a tough one. The fish is able to use its bulk and slab-sided build to put a lot of pressure on fine fly tackle. It can be quite an unexpected thrill.

There is another fish carrying the bream name – the so-called silver bream. Its distribution is wide and its preferred habitat is identical to that of the common bream. However, this fish is a totally different variety, even though it is a very close relative. The general shape is somewhat similar but the coloration is always completely silver. It is also a very much smaller fish, rarely exceeding 0.5 kg (1 lb). The diet of the silver bream is basically the same as that of the common bream, except that it will rarely be found in mid-water and shows no interest in chasing fish fry. If the flyfisher accidentally takes this fish it will be whilst fishing a weighted wet fly or nymph very close to the bottom for other quarry.

Carp are also of several varieties but mirror carp, common carp and crucian carp are those most commonly encountered.

Their distribution is very wide and their usual habitat is slow-moving rivers, lakes, ponds, reservoirs and canals. It is a source of wonder that extremely large fish are often encountered in very small waters.

It is well known that the common carp and the mirror carp can grow to colossal weights (the crucian carp is a very much smaller fish). Carp have been caught on rod and line in excess of 18 kg (40 lb), but this has always been on bait fished by specialist carp anglers, very often during the hours of darkness.

The following actual incident will give an insight into the flyfishing potential of carp.

It happened while I was flyfishing for trout on a small private lake during a midsummer day. The lake was known to hold a number of good-sized brown trout, several in the 3 kg (6–7 lb) class.

There were several dense reed beds growing along the edge of the lake and I heard (rather than saw) a disturbance close to the edge of a nearby one. I watched carefully for a few minutes to locate the activity and saw what appeared to be the back of a good-sized brown trout slightly break the water surface. I quickly changed my fly to a weighted Gold-Ribbed Hare's Ear nymph and cast beyond and close to the reeds so as to retrieve the nymph alongside the reed bed, but just under the surface.

After a few slow hand-twist retrieves I felt a solid pull and immediately tightened to set the hook. Before I could fully grasp what was happening, my flyrod was bent into a huge hoop and the flyline was cutting through the water like a knife, dragging out yards of backing behind it, as the fish made a direct and fast run out into the lake.

Yes, the fish *was* eventually landed, even though the trout landing net proved totally inadequate for the job and sustained substantial damage. It turned out to be a mirror carp of 7.5 kg (16 lb 9 oz) and it was taken on a 3x leader and a size 14 GRHE.

This was certainly not an everyday happening (unfortunately), but it does demonstrate the potential of flyfishing for coarse fish, and the unexpected encounter that is sometimes the memorable result.

## Chapter 9

# *The Wet Fly*

Fish have been caught on lures made from feathers since ancient times, and in medieval England the use of trout flies was not unknown. We have drawings of flies in use during the fifteenth century, and they are remarkably similar to the wet flies used today. The descriptions of the materials used show considerable

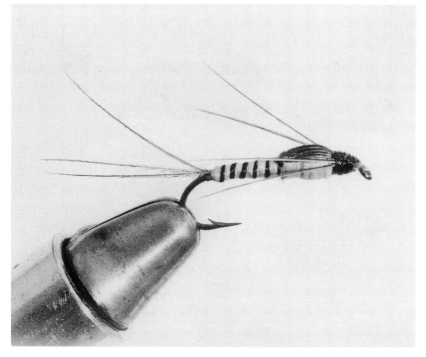

*A typical American nymph*

insight into the trout's feeding habits, and point to the attention these early anglers paid to materials in order to obtain a measure of imitation.

Have modern developments given us a better fly? In some instances they have, for a wider choice of materials is available, with better hooks and flytying tools contributing to a construction that is vastly superior to those flies of long ago. On the other hand, many of the materials used today, especially the synthetics, are not nearly as good for this purpose as the furs and hairs used by our predecessors. There has also been the American influence, for hundreds of fly patterns have crossed the Atlantic to find favour with British anglers.

It must be borne in mind that the American flies have mainly been designed to take American native trout – brook trout and rainbow trout – and these fish are notoriously naïve compared with our native browns. One of the reasons for the ready acceptance of so many American patterns has been the advent of reservoir fishing for rainbow trout, because, apart from the traditional loch flies, there were no suitable patterns for this type

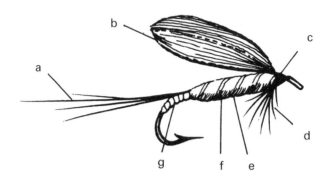

*Fig. 17 The parts of a wet fly*
*A – Tail, B – Wing, C – Head, D – Throat Hackle, E – Ribbing, F – Body, G – Tag*

of fishing. But the river angler, fishing for native browns, should exercise the utmost caution when considering the use of American flies; many of our own traditional patterns are vastly superior.

Today, the use of colour in the design of wet flies almost defies description. Without any difficulty whatever, a list of over 500 wet flies could be compiled, containing almost every colour known to man – and no two would have the same dressing! It must be asked: are they all necessary?

To add to the confusion of all these colours, flies are tied to different designs. Even the various regions of the UK have traditional basic patterns which are tied in various combinations of colour and materials (see fig. 18).

In order to make any sense out of this multitude of wet flies, it is necessary to have a very clear understanding of what we are trying to achieve when we use them. First and foremost, we are attempting to offer to the fish an object that gives the illusion of food. The problem is, what food? If we are absolutely honest with ourselves we must admit that we just do not know. It is possible that, each time a wet fly is taken during a day's fishing, the reason is different; each time it momentarily created the illusion of a different food form, and we never know for certain what that food form was.

While the wet fly is in the water it behaves according to the many influences exerted on it. These influences may be the result of the current, underwater obstructions, the weighting of the fly, the restriction of the line, or the type of manipulation employed by the angler. During each cast the fly might well behave in several different ways as each influence is brought to bear. At times the fly might represent a drowned terrestrial fly being carried along by the current; at other times it might give the illusion of a darting nymph. Then again, it might present the perfect illusion of a swimming fish fry, or the normal passage of an underwater insect such as a beetle. If it rises to the surface during its traverse it may have the action of a hatching aquatic fly.

a) North Country

b) Southern Counties

c) Wales

d) West Country

e) Welsh Usk

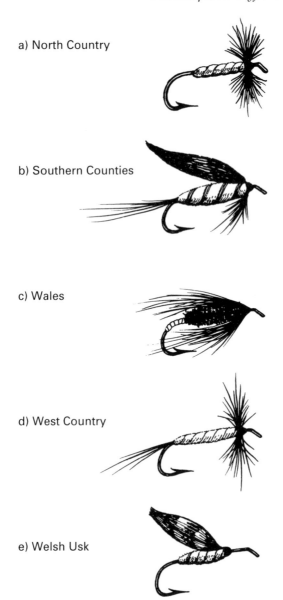

*Fig. 18 Regional wet flies*

Now we can begin to see why the multitude of different wet flies have all been successful at various times under different conditions. However, duplicating those conditions is a different matter, and it is necessary to look into the problem a little deeper before making a selection for the fly box.

Our first consideration must be the type of fish we expect to encounter. As previously mentioned, the wild brownie is not, normally, attracted by flies tied in primary colours. The dace has a penchant for small black flies, the chub has a preference for a 'buggy' offering, while the rainbow trout and the perch will both take flies tied in primary colours. This knowledge automatically whittles down the selection process quite significantly. So now let us look into the matter of deception.

The fast, often turbulent waters of the North and West Country require a fly that has a 'kick', that is to say, the hackle should be sparse and tied similar to a dry fly so that it may be agitated by the fast water. The mostly serene waters of the southern counties are better fished with a 'standard' wet fly. The heavily wooded Welsh valleys result in waters that abound in small terrestrials, and the regional patterns reflect this with their fur and herl bodies. So, regional patterns also help in our selection process.

If the water we intend to fish has stretches, runs, or holes of good depth, we may well decide to fish deep down using a weighted fly. A lot of weight is not necessary; it will make the fly difficult to cast and impair its natural movement in the water. A little lead tied in under the hook shank is vastly superior to pinching a weight onto the leader (see fig. 19). We should certainly have a few weighted patterns in our box.

Leaders should enter a discussion about the use of weighted flies. Never try to cast a weighted fly unless you have a fairly robust tippet to your leader – it is surprising how even a lightly weighted fly can snap a tippet during casting. Also, when fishing deep, you should use a sinkant on your leader and fly. The best procedure is to apply the solution to the leader and then, while it dries, add a little to the fly, lightly rinsing it before use.

The materials with which the fly is tied have a large bearing on the illusion it will create. Synthetic material does very little to help us. The texture and colour may look attractive to the angler – and they are certainly easy to use – but bodies tied with fur, hair, or feather fibre create a totally different illusion under water. The natural materials trap tiny air bubbles in the fibres that create a translucent, silvery sheen when submerged, very similar to the appearance of a natural insect. In fact, many small underwater insects breathe by carrying around with them a minute bubble of air. Wool, for the same reason as synthetics, is also a poor material for a wet fly – it has a dead appearance in the water. Wool is sometimes used because it sinks a fly so well, and it is available in such a wide range of colours, but the draw-

Fine lead wire in coils: used when heavy weighting is required, e.g. lures.

Fine lead wire strip: better weighting for a wet fly dressing.

*Fig. 19 To weight a wet fly or lure*

backs outweigh the advantages, for even the colours are not stable when wet.

Exact colour is not necessary in a wet fly and, in any case, it is nearly impossible to duplicate nature's own colours. Also, what are we trying to duplicate? Since we are not that sure of the food form we are attempting to simulate, it is far more important that we attempt to create a general illusion of several different forms of food.

The angler must remember, too, that the fly has motion in the water when it is being manipulated, and different materials used for the wings can produce varied effects (see fig. 20). If the standard quill feather wing is replaced with a bunch of hackle fibres, the fly will have motion even in slack water; the weight of the water alone will undulate the fine fibres in a lifelike, pulsating way. A hair wing will have the same action in heavier water. The use of fibres from duck or teal breast feathers creates a wonderful hazy illusion of movement, their broken colour and fine texture combining to give this impression even in slack water.

Tinsel is used in a wet fly for many reasons. It most certainly gives 'flash' and the impression of movement, and this is particularly attractive to rainbows and perch. It also helps create the illusion of a small fish fry – a quick flash of silver is sometimes the only indication of their presence. But there is another use for tinsel that is not widely appreciated. Many underwater insects are not only translucent, but their hard shell-like bodies have a reflective quality, and their true colour is influenced by the surroundings and by air bubbles lodged in their body. A semi-translucent nymph, of general brown coloration, may well show tones of green reflected from underwater plant life in the vicinity.

My 'Reflector Nymph' (fig. 21), was designed to take advantage of this. The body is of flat gold tinsel with a ribbing of oval gold tinsel, the whole being given several coats of clear lacquer; a stubby wing and a long tail of duck or teal fibres complete the fly. The result is an artificial fly with a general nymph outline

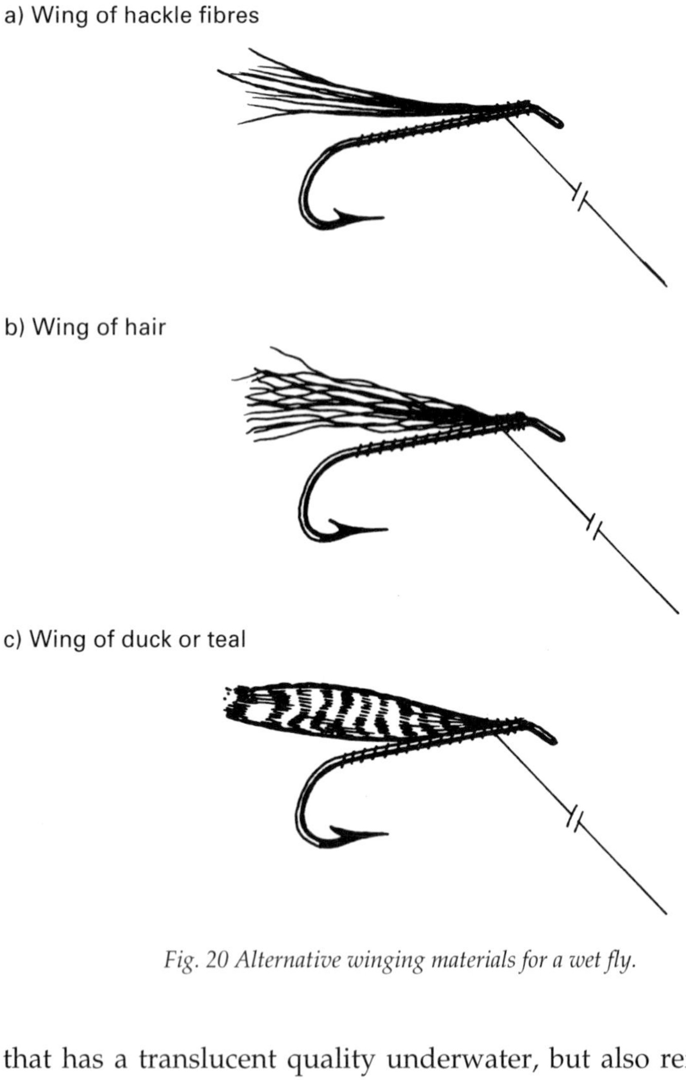

a) Wing of hackle fibres

b) Wing of hair

c) Wing of duck or teal

*Fig. 20 Alternative winging materials for a wet fly.*

that has a translucent quality underwater, but also reflects the surrounding brown rocks, stones or green plant life. It has proved to be a killing pattern for wild brownies. For instance, during one summer evening it took 11 browns in a couple of hours' fishing, all from the same pool!

If tinsel is used in a standard dressing, it should not overdress the fly. Use fine flat tinsel for ribbing in fairly open turns so that plenty of body material shows through – fine oval tinsel or gold wire is even better. Mylar tinsel, a reasonably new material, is now available in fine, narrow widths and it can be obtained in a reversible form, gold one side, silver the other. It has the advantage that it does not tarnish. Although not as tough as metallic tinsel, it will give good service and is very easy to use.

It is difficult to give advice on the size of wet flies. So much depends on the size of fish expected, the colour of the water, the brightness of the day, and so on. As a general rule, use one or two sizes larger than would be used for a dry fly under similar conditions, and a little larger still if the light is poor or the water coloured. This advice may sound confusing – after all, what is the correct size for a dry fly? (Fortunately, this is a little more

*The Reflector Nymph*

standard, and will be discussed in detail in a later chapter.) Returning to the subject of wet fly size, it is sometimes surprising how large a fly will be confidently taken underwater – a feeding fish feels somewhat safer in its own environment below the surface.

Particular attention should be paid to the storage of wet flies before and after use, and between seasons. Flies are nearly

a) Standard Nymph dressing

Note the fur body and thorax to give an irregular outline. A wing-case is tied over the thorax. Tail is long.

b) Reflector Nymph

My own pattern, dressed with a tinsel body to reflect the underwater environment, then a ribbing of oval tinsel. Wing and tail of duck fibres.

*Fig. 21 Nymph patterns*

always returned to the fly box while still wet, where they are hooked into a lining material that holds water – the result is RUST. A hook that is rusty will discolour the dressing, tarnish any tinsel, corrode the eye and, worst of all, damage the barb. Try to remember to hook used flies into the fly-patch on your fishing waistcoat, so that they can dry off before being returned to the box. Also, periodically inspect all your flies and sharpen the barbs with a fine stone during each inspection, whether they obviously need it or not.

Between seasons the danger is the common clothes moth. For some reason, flies seem very attractive to them, I do not know how they get into a closed and stored fly box, but they do. Many a fly box has been opened at the beginning of a season to reveal nothing but bare hooks. Before you store your box at the end of the season, always add a few crystals of moth deterrent – it will make the flies smelly, but the fish never seem to notice.

## Fishing the wet fly

The wet fly can be fished upstream, downstream, cross-stream, down deep, and 'sweeping' a pool. Each method has variations in technique that can be incorporated as required.

The most commonly used is the downstream method, although it is not necessarily the best under all conditions. On some waters, the use of a wet fly downstream is forbidden, and I have never really understood the reason for this rule. The usual explanation is that a wet fly fished downstream has a tendency to attract the smaller trout, but this has not been borne out by experience. It is difficult to see the difference between a wet fly in free drift downstream, and one that is drifting down towards the angler from upstream, but rules must be obeyed, and if we dislike them we should not fish the water.

The downstream cast (see fig. 22), is usually made across stream, quartering down. When the fly enters the water at X a little slack line is immediately given so that the fly is in free drift to point A. During this stage no motion is given to the fly by the

angler, if necessary additional slack may be given to increase the
distance between X and A. On reaching A the fly is allowed to
swing across the current to B on a tight line. During the free drift
the fly has usually sunk to a low level, the swing from A to B
being made in a rising arc until at B the fly is almost at the
surface. The fly is then retrieved by the angler in short pulls, first
to point C, then D, then E, then F. The fly is then recast to another
point, X, and the procedure repeated. After several such casts,
the angler will move a few paces downstream to fish new water.
The roll cast is particularly useful in this type of fishing.

Variations consist of allowing the fly to sink to various depths,
manipulating the fly during the free drift, and in variations of
the retrieve between points B and F. A take during the free drift

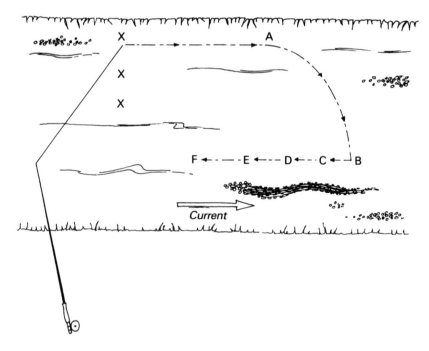

*Fig. 22 Standard downstream wet fly cast*

is usually very gentle, sometimes the indication is a mere twitch of the line or leader, but during the swinging, rising arc and the periods of retrieve the take is much more decisive, usually felt by a good pull.

The upstream method is more suited to a nymph pattern, but a wet fly is also effective. The cast is made directly, or quartering upstream, and the fly allowed to be carried by the current back to the angler. No manipulation by the angler is needed except to draw in the slack line as the fly progresses downstream. Often the fly can be allowed to continue downstream to complete a swinging arc at the end of the cast. This method allows a natural drift downstream that is very attractive to the fish. Takes are quite hard to detect and the line should be watched most carefully. Any twitch of the line or momentary pause in its movement downstream should result in an instantaneous strike from the angler. To vary the upstream cast, a weighted fly can be used that will sink very quickly and be rolled along the stream bed by the current. This technique is particularly effective at the head of pools.

The cross-stream method is usually combined with fishing very deep, and is a particularly good way to reach those fish that lie in deep holes, or close to undercut banks. The fly used, nearly always one that has been weighted, is cast across and a little upstream to allow it time to sink to the bottom before it reaches the fish. The farther upstream it is cast, the greater the depth at which it will be when it arrives at the hole. Usually, no manipulation of the fly is necessary as fish that lie deep are accustomed to their food being washed down to them in this manner. The take may be either gentle or quite savage; keep a straight line and respond immediately a fish is felt.

'Sweeping' a pool is done so that all water in the pool is covered at all depths. It is a particularly useful technique when fishing very early in the morning or late in the evening; at these times the fish may be anywhere in the pool and on the feed. The method can also be used when the water is on the high side and a little coloured – the fish are very often found in open water during such conditions. One of the advantages of this method is that almost no casting is required, and there is consequently little disturbance to the water.

The 'sweeping' operation is considerably easier to perform than to describe, but I hope that the following description – together with a study of fig. 23 – will enable you to try it for yourself. The first thing to remember is that the same length of line is used throughout, no motion is imparted to the fly by the angler, and the fly remains in the water at all times. Commence operations by placing yourself as close as possible to the stream centre, facing downstream. Make your initial cast to X (fig. 23) and allow the current to carry the fly to A. Raise the rod so that the fly is drawn upstream to B, then flip a curved belly of line to the right. The fly will be taken by the current to C, then, still carried by the current, will swing to D. The first 'sweep' has now been completed.

Without removing the fly from the water the angler takes a couple of paces downstream to commence the next 'sweep'. Again the rod is raised to draw the fly upstream, and this time a curved belly of line is flipped to the left. After the fly has made the traverse to the left and returned to centre stream, the rod is again raised and a curved belly of line flipped to the right. When the fly is once again at stream centre the second 'sweep' has been completed. The process is repeated down the length of the pool.

In this manner the fly is made to search the entire pool in a series of sweeping arcs. At various times during the operation the fly is worked at different depths, and there is an element of retrieve upstream which is also attractive. The bonus is that the fly is always in the water, where it will do the most good.

You may be interested in the origin of this method of fishing the wet fly. Some years ago, I was fishing with a companion in the Catskill Mountains, USA. It had been a poor morning with very little to show for a lot of hard work. As we sat on the river bank having our lunch, we watched two small boys fishing. Neither of the boys was casting; they just let their flies play in the

# The Wet Fly

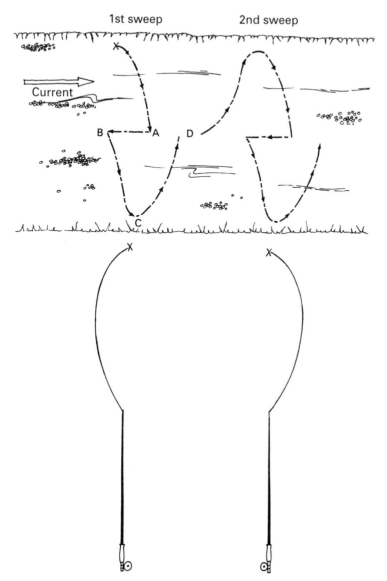

Fig. 23 'Sweeping' a pool
At the end of each complete 'sweep' the angler moves forward a couple of paces. Line is
drawn in, then a curved belly of line is flipped first to one side, then to the other, in
order to complete a new 'sweep'.

current below them, and now and again drew the flies towards them and allowed the current to swing the flies across the stream. The important part of this story is that they were catching fish – quite a number of fish! So, if anyone ever asks who the originator of this method was, the answer is two small boys in the Catskills!

# Chapter 10

# Natural Flies and Imitations

Most natural insects that find themselves on the water surface are liable to be taken as food by naturally surface-feeding fish. Flies form a large proportion of such food and these may be water-bred or terrestrial.

It would be impossible in a book of this size to cover in depth all natural flies, their life cycles, identification characteristics, and so on. There exist many excellent reference books that may be studied if the angler wishes to enlarge his knowledge of entomology. The purpose of this chapter is to indicate the general pattern of insects that may be expected at any particular time, and to offer basic guidance as to the artificial that may be used to imitate the natural.

Of course, there are many more patterns of artificials than will be discussed here – and it cannot be claimed that the selection I give will necessarily be the best – but it is hoped it will be the basis for a fly box that will be useful throughout the season. To list all the artificial patterns available would require much more space than is available, which applies also to the various dressings. It is certain that, after reading this chapter, many knowledgeable anglers will immediately query the exclusion of a favourite artificial that has proved itself over and over again – and, of course, they are right. As time goes by, anglers will add many more artificials to their fly box than will be mentioned here, and their short-list of favourites is bound to emerge.

Now, a word of caution. Most fishermen carry far too large a selection of flies. Far better to have a good basic selection, plus one or two favourites, and to persevere with these, rather than be forever changing flies. Only a fly on the water will catch fish; time spent changing flies unnecessarily is lost fishing time, particularly during a short-duration hatch of naturals. It is better to make an educated choice in the first place, then concentrate on the presentation.

Apart from terrestrial insects, which we shall discuss later, most natural flies fall into one of the following Orders.

*1 Ephemeroptera* These are water-bred flies of the mayfly type. They have four wings which are carried in the upright position. At first glance only the two large front wings may be apparent; the two rear wings are small by comparison. The life-cycle passes through three stages: the egg, the nymphal stage, and the perfect fly, referred to as the imago. The hatched fly will be first a dun (sub-imago), then later moult to a spinner (imago), and can be male or female. Duns have dull-coloured wings, whereas the spinner's wings are perfectly clear. Male duns or spinners have large, coloured eyes, and claspers under the body for holding the female during mating. The tails are very long, often twice the length of the fly. Female duns and spinners have very small eyes, no claspers under the body, and their tails are quite short, often only the length of the fly.

Hatched duns moult to spinners before mating takes place in the air and above the water. After mating, and depending on the species, the female spinner will lay its eggs, either underwater on plant life or stones, or on the water, or drop them to the water surface. After egg-laying, many female spinners will be found dead or 'spent' on the water surface. The spinner's coloration and appearance is somewhat different from the hatching dun, usually more delicate and lighter-coloured, and in many cases a different colour entirely. Fish will feed on both the hatching duns and the 'spent' spinners.

There are approximately 40 known species of Ephemeroptera,

and they vary in size and coloration to a considerable degree. Included in this species are those flies commonly called large dark olives, medium olives, blue-winged olives, pale wateries, iron blues, march browns, yellow mays and, of course, the mayfly.

2 *Trichoptera* These are the sedge, caddis, and grannom flies. They have two pairs of wings which are slightly hairy, and are carried folded back and closed in what may be described as 'tent' or 'roof' style. These flies have no tails. There are over 100 species of Trichoptera, of which only four or five are of real interest to the angler. They vary considerably in size and coloration.

3 *Pleuroptera* These are the alder-type flies. They have two pairs of delicately veined wings which are carried closed and folded back in similar fashion to the sedges. Another prominent feature is the large head which carries two antennae. They have no tails. There are only two alder flies, both *Sialis* species.

4 *Plecoptera* The willow-type flies are of the Perlidae family. They have four narrow wings, folded back and carried flat over the body. They vary in size and coloration, but are easy to distinguish from the Trichoptera and the Pleuroptera due to the position of the wings. Numerous flies fall into this category, and many are of no interest to the angler as they are rarely on the surface of the water – in some cases the nymph crawls out of the water before hatching into the adult fly.

5 *Diptera* These flies are similar in appearance to the common house fly, but vary in size tremendously. They have only two wings. There are over 5,000 British species of true flies in this Order, many of which are terrestrial and rarely fly over water. Other terrestrials are often attracted by the water. They all have one thing in common: they are small. The flies often referred to as smuts, gnats and midges are found in this Order.

It is of considerable help to the angler when trying to identify natural flies if he has a fair idea of what may be expected at various times of the day or season. Even if flies are not apparent and general prospecting is in order, it still helps if the artificial selected matches the fly that might be expected by the fish. Fish are often selective while a hatch is actually taking place, and at that time it is essential to use the correct artificial. Even when there is no hatch, fish are inclined to be wary of fly patterns that have no place on the water at that time. They may not associate with food artificials that bear no resemblance to the flies recently seen.

It would be impossible to specify the particular fly that could be on the water at a certain time of the day, or during a particular part of the season. Fly hatches are influenced by water and air temperatures, weather pressure systems, and whether the day is bright or dull, cold or windy. There is also a considerable overlapping between species. However, the following, if taken in a general sense, might be a useful guide.

Very early in the season, when it is often quite cold, fly hatches (in fact any form of fly life) are not that common. However, even in quite cold weather the march brown will appear. This is one of our very large flies and easy to identify with its brown body and fawn-coloured wings. At such times, prospecting with a dry fly is not very rewarding, and the use of terrestrial patterns is almost useless. It is a different matter during a hatch of march browns, and good sport will often result. The hatches are usually of a short duration, but several may occur during the midday period.

April brings some improvement. March browns may still be encountered, and this is the month of the large dark olive. This insect is also easy to identify, due to its dark olive-coloured body. It has smoky blue-grey wings and is quite large. Hatches are inclined to be more prolific than with the march brown, and again take place during the midday period. Fish at this time of the year are normally lean and hungry and the hatches of large olives are greedily attacked. The grannom and silver sedge also make their appearance at this time of the year, and a few medium olives may be expected.

During the early spring, march browns become rare, large dark olives are still encountered, but it is time for the medium olive. This is a smaller fly than the large olive, and is usually lighter olive in colour, but colours vary enormously from water to water, and sometimes between flies. Grannom, silver sedge and black gnats are also evident at this time of year.

May will bring the hatches of iron blues, especially if the weather is cold. When examined closely, the iron blue's name is clearly accurate, but from a distance the fly appears to be almost black. Olives are still on the water, particularly the medium olive, and during the evenings sedges will appear, especially at dusk. Black gnats become more plentiful, and if the weather is warm a few pale wateries may be seen late in the day.

The summer months begin to bring an end to the midday hatches. Iron blues and olives are still inclined to hatch on colder days, but not to the same extent, and pale wateries will now be more obvious. Sedges are also plentiful in early evening. Spinners are over the water laying eggs during the day, and rising fish may well be taking 'spent' spinners from the water surface. Most hatches are now taking place during the early evening and terrestrials are quite plentiful.

The tail of the season brings the return of black gnats, sometimes in gigantic numbers. Olives and pale wateries are still about, although during the day it may well be the 'spent' spinner that attracts interest. Towards the very end of the season large dark olives may reappear, especially if there is a decided drop in temperature. Generally speaking, flies are not that abundant, but fish are quite active and prospecting likely lies brings good results.

Now comes the difficult task of selecting artificials to represent these natural flies – there are so many patterns to choose from. The following list may help establish a *basic* fly box to which the angler can add as time goes by.

| Natural | Artificial |
|---|---|
| Large dark olive | Dark Olive, Blue Upright, Gold-ribbed Hare's Ear (Spinner: Large Red Spinner) |
| Medium olive | Medium Olive, Rough Olive, Gold-ribbed Hare's Ear, Greenwell's Glory (Spinner: Lunn's Particular) |
| Blue-winged olive | Blue-Winged Olive (Spinner: Sherry Spinner) |
| Pale wateries | Tup's Indispensable, Blue Quill, Pale Watery (Spinner: Amber Spinner) |
| Iron blues | Iron Blue (Spinner: Houghton Ruby or Jenny Spinner) |
| March brown | March Brown (Spinner: a much lighter-coloured fly) |
| Sedges | Brown Sedge, Silver Sedge, Welshman's Button. |
| Alders Willow flies Black gnats | Standard patterns |

## Chapter 11

# The Dry Fly

When compared with the wet fly, the dry fly is a comparatively new innovation. It is believed that as early as the eighteenth century, experiments were taking place with the dry fly, and certainly the interest had reached its peak during the latter part of the 1800s. On the British side of the Atlantic anglers like Maryatt and Halford did much to establish the credentials of the dry fly and, after correspondence with Halford, Gordon and Hewitt did the same in the America.

The early dry fly was little more than a wet fly that had been dressed to float, and as the floatability was still far from satisfactory, mixtures of kerosene and paraffin-wax were used to anoint the fly. The main problem in the UK was the intense determination to imitate the natural, using materials that hampered the floating capabilities of the fly. In the USA, a slightly different approach, aiming to create an 'illusion' of the natural, made progress a little easier. Gordon used quill bodies for his flies, and Hewitt attempted to create purely optical illusions.

Very soon quill bodies were in use on both sides of the Atlantic, and dubbed bodies of fur or hair lost some of their popularity. The evolution of the dry fly suffered from these diverse opinions, and the intense desire to arrive at exact imitation certainly slowed development.

Today, the controversy over exact imitation versus optical illusion is still with us. In the past this controversy was waged in print by the contestants. It has now reached the stage where there are two distinct schools of thought. In these pages we are more concerned with the illusion aspect, for no matter how strong the desire for exact imitations may be, it must be accepted that it is not within the capabilities of man to produce an exact copy of nature.

No matter how studiously colours are matched, or how carefully materials are selected, the imitation dry fly is a very poor copy of the natural, and even more so when the hook is taken into consideration. A dry fly has to be dressed so as to float the hook and, consequently, in no way does it resemble the general outline of a natural insect. If we are prepared to accept that a fish has good eyesight, and is completely familiar with the appearance of natural flies, then we must concentrate on presenting an optical illusion that will deceive it. One day exact imitation may become possible, and we should all work towards that goal – in the meantime we have fish to catch.

We know that fish regularly take the artificials we offer, we know that these artificials are not exact imitations of any natural insect, and we are also aware of the excellent eyesight of the fish. So why are our artificials taken? Let us try to reach a conclusion that will help us to catch fish.

In the first instance, it must be borne in mind that the fish does not see the dry fly in its own environment, but views the imitation through a broken water surface. In fact, the view is first through water, then through the broken surface film, and then through air. The question must be asked: does the fish see any fly on the surface that clearly? It is suggested that it does not, seeing only the indentations in the surface film caused by the legs of the natural, or the hackle points of the artificial. The rest of the insect is no more than an indistinct form. The colour of the hazy image *might* have some significance, the size is obviously quite important, but the most important of all is the general outline.

Colour must be considered an unknown quantity. We have no reason to believe that the fish is able to see colours exactly as we do, although there is evidence that trout are better than people at discriminating colours at the red and blue ends of the spectrum. All we can do is to present a fly that has a colour in keeping with the predominant colour of the natural – 'predominant' because the colour of a natural is not always readily apparent, very often the underlying colour is the most predominant.

In order to create an artificial that will present a good 'hazy' impression of a natural, a great deal of work has gone into the design of the general form. Many different styles of dressing are now used, and some have become firmly established as proven takers of fish.

A standard winged dry fly is shown in fig. 24, with the same fly dressed 'buzz' style without the wings. In the early days all dry flies were dressed with wings; the slavish attention to exact imitation did not allow any alternative. The 'hackle' or 'buzz' fly followed very quickly and proved itself fully effective, and much easier to use on rough water. Fig. 24 also shows a fly tied in the 'balanced' manner. In this type of dressing a slightly longer hook shank (2x) is used, and the fly tied on the rear three-quarters of the shank. The Toronto Flytyers' Club of Canada originated this design. The fly cocks beautifully on the water, and the hooking power of the fly is considerably improved.

The 'thorax' dressing in fig. 25 was developed in the USA for use on limestone waters, the equivalent of our chalk streams. The hackle is tied in figure-of-eight manner, very central on the shank; the floatability is excellent, only the hackle points ever touch the water. The thorax style also allows a longer hook shank to be used, so in a way it is also a balanced fly with improved hooking power.

The Stubby-Wing Variant (fig. 25) is the standard variant dressing as favoured by the American anglers. In fact, the size of the wings is normal; it is the hackle which is tied over-size. The body of these flies is usually quill, and the hackle multi-coloured, created by using two hackle feathers of different colours, or using just one feather that is either grizzle or cree. These flies ride very high on the water to give an excellent 'hazy' impression of a natural, and their colour combination is usually

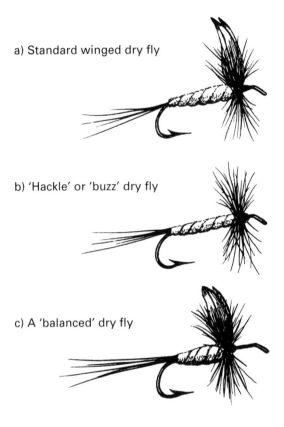

a) Standard winged dry fly

b) 'Hackle' or 'buzz' dry fly

c) A 'balanced' dry fly

*Fig. 24. Dry fly variations*

that of two natural flies, both of which could be expected on the water at the time the variant is used.

The High-Wing Variant (fig. 25) has the same basic dressing as the Standard-Wing Variant, except that the wing is tied very high – one and a half times the length of the hook shank – and usually consists of a bunch of duck or teal breast feather fibres;

*The High-Wing Variant*

there is no need for the wing to be divided. This design is my own; it has all the advantages of the standard variant, plus the added bonus of the high wing coming into the fish's field of vision much earlier. It has been very successful when used for wild brownies.

The Spider Fly, and the Neversink Skater (see fig. 26), although appearing different, have the same background. Both flies originated in the USA and are superb examples of the 'hazy optical illusion' theory. The Neversink Skater was the first of the duo, designed by Hewitt for use on the Neversink River, Catskill

a) Dry fly with 'thorax' dressing

b) 'Stubby-Wing Variant'

c) 'High-Wing Variant'

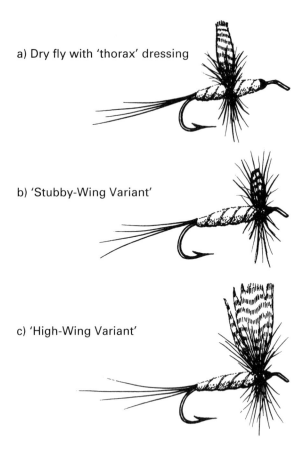

*Fig. 25 Dry fly variations*

Mountains Region. Having such an oversized hackle, and no tail, the small hook hangs downwards in the water with the hackle spread over the surface. From the point of view of the fish there is just no fly to be seen, just a circle of surface indentations caused by the hackle points. This fly is outstandingly successful on smooth glassy glides of water, especially in bright sunlight.

The Spider Fly is simply a Neversink Skater tied with a long tail. The tail enables the fly to ride the water in the normal way, but very high with the hook well out of the surface film. The small body of the Spider is usually of gold tinsel to catch the sun. It is designed to be used under the same conditions as the Skater, and is one of the most effective flies in bright sunlight. I have carried out many experiments with this fly, using various colour combinations at different times of the day, and have found that a white-hackled Spider is extremely effective on a summer evening as dusk approaches.

Flies for coarse fish (see fig. 27) need a different approach. The chub flies, the Cat-Bug and the Bumble, are designed to meet the requirement of a 'good mouthful', and at the same time give the general impression of terrestrials that often fall onto the water.

a) Standard Spider Fly

b) 'Neversink Skater' (named after the Neversink River, Catskill Mountains, USA)

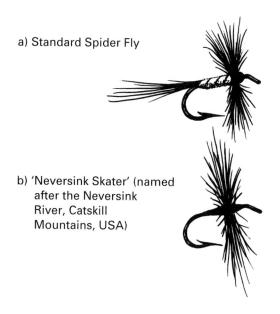

*Fig. 26 Dry fly variations*

95

Both flies are intended to be fished lying in the surface film. The Cat-Bug has a body of black ostrich herl, tied on the fat side, with a hackle of grizzle tied palmer. It gives a fair impression of a fat caterpillar and is often greedily taken. The Bumble is intended to represent one of those species of flies that have a black-and-yellow striped body. However, this is only a loose description as the fly is tied quite large (size 10 hook), and the head of peacock herl makes the fly decidedly plump. The striped body is constructed by winding alternative turns of yellow and black fine chenille.

The dace fly, the Black Gnat (also shown in fig. 27), is tied on a hook no larger than size 18, preferably a size 20. The simple body is of black tying silk, the tail black, and the palmer hackle black. When tying such a small fly, the problem is usually the hackle – it is very difficult to find a hackle small enough. The answer is to use the smallest hackle feather you have, then to trim it to size with scissors after it is tied in. Not a very elegant way to tie flies – but the dace do not object!

Except where indicated otherwise, the hook size of a dry fly is dictated by the size of the natural it imitates. True, we often use a larger fly when the light is fading, or at night, but this is pure 'angler's licence' for improved visibility – for the fish as well as the angler. The professional flytiers offer each fly pattern in several sizes, and it is very difficult to understand why, for the difference between size 12 and size 18 flies is considerable, very much more than the variation in size between the naturals. Even worse, the flies are often 'tied' the same size, only the hook is different. It is most important that flies are tied relative to the hook size; anything else should be firmly rejected.

Only during the short mayfly season are we likely to see natural flies that need to be represented by a size 12 imitation. In the USA and Canada this is not always the case, and several early season flies are quite large, but in the UK we have no equivalent of these. During the UK season practically all naturals can be represented by artificials tied on hooks of sizes 14–18. There are, of course, many naturals which are usually classified as midges, and these are best portrayed on hook sizes 20 and 22. The term 'midge' is merely a general term and refers to a group of small flies, many of whose naturals are legitimate aquatic flies, while others are terrestrials attracted by the water.

There was once an adage among bait fishermen: 'big fish, big hook!' but this is not true where flies are concerned. The angler is trying to create an illusion of a natural, and naturals do not vary their size according to the size of the fish. Quite large fish will greedily take a natural that can only be imitated on a size 16 hook. Never worry about the hook holding firm; only in exceptional circumstances will you ever lose a wild brownie because of the hook size. I have personal experience of a 4 kg (9 lb) trout that lost the fight against a size 16 hook. The flyfisher's problem

a) Cat-Bug – chub fly

b) Bumble – chub fly

c) Black Gnat – dace fly

*Fig. 27 Coarse fish flies*

is not the small hook size, but the fine tippets that have to be used to cast these flies. *Never* economise when you purchase nylon tippet material – only the best will do!

The materials used to create dry flies are too numerous to be intelligently discussed in these pages, but a few general observations may be of practical help.

Body material receives more attention than it deserves, since our intention should be to present a minimal view of any body material to the fish. The natural insect, unless it is spent and lying in the surface film, usually carries its body curved upwards away from the water, added to which it is often translucent, and in any case, we only wish to present an illusion. The body of a good dry fly should be negligible, and preferably not opaque. Quills certainly make a small, neat body and do not soak up water, but they are not translucent and give a hard outline when seen in silhouette. Dubbed bodies of fur or hair, provided the dubbing is kept sparse, are vastly superior and almost create a translucent effect when viewed against the light. Wool must never be used, for quite apart from the dead colour, it soaks up water like a sponge.

Many nicely tied dry flies are completely spoilt by the tail. The tail of a natural fly cannot be represented by a bunch of, probably, 10 or 12 hackle fibres, tied so that they lie close together. This type of tail is usually tied by anglers who believe that it helps the fly to float. It certainly does not. No matter how well such a tail is treated with floatant, it still soaks up water by capillary action, and in fact will help sink the fly. Using just two or three wisps is a much better idea, but rather difficult to achieve if the material used is hackle fibre. This problem can be overcome by using the guard hairs from certain animals, hairs that are on the stiff side and easily tied. Polar bear is a typical example, and a maximum of three hairs should be used. I have sometimes used bristles from a decorating brush and found them to be excellent material.

The American idea of using duck or teal breast feather fibres to create wings is excellent. Wings of quill feather always become separated and tatty in use, so why not use separate fibres in the first place? Duck or teal fibres are so easy to tie in, and a small bunch separate easily into two wings with a couple of figure-of-eight turns of tying silk. The resulting wings have a 'broken' appearance that simulates movement and helps create that hazy illusion we seek.

Only first-quality cock hackles should be used to hackle a dry fly, and the fibres should be stiff, sharp and shiny. These days such hackles are expensive, and the constant complaint is the shortage of small hackles. Most cock capes have sufficient hackles of the correct size, but for some unknown reason they are considered too short. This is not so; a small hackle does not have to be long to give four windings – and that is all that is required, while there is even better.

## Fishing the dry fly

Fishing the dry fly is considerably easier than wet fly fishing – that is to say, it is considerably easier than fishing a wet fly skilfully and well. Far too many anglers consider the dry fly to be something very special and hesitate to use it except on very odd occasions. There are times when nothing else will do, and we should all feel confident in our ability to use it.

The dry fly has the advantage that we can always see exactly what is happening; it does not have to be worked and manipulated into fish lies, nor do we have to concern ourselves with detecting very subtle takes. The dry fly technique is basically simple in concept; we have only to create the illusion of a floating insect being carried by the current without hindrance. The difficulties which have to be overcome are threefold: we have to present an illusion that is acceptable to the fish, it has to be a delicate presentation so as not to frighten the fish, and it must be presented in such a manner that it floats freely without being dragged in the current by the line and leader.

It is standard practice to fish a dry fly upstream and, although downstream fishing is possible – and sometimes necessary – the first choice should always be to fish upstream as it is much easier. To fish upstream does not mean directly upstream, but at an angle across and up. If you fish directly upstream, your line or leader will pass over every fish that sees the fly – it is not to be thought about!

Before casting, make sure that your fly is well treated with a suitable floatant, of which there are many different types on the market. The best is possibly a liquid preparation that contains silicone into which the fly can be dipped. The spray cans of floatant are quite effective but very wasteful, and powder floatants are not suitable for the initial treatment of flies. After dipping, blow on the fly to dry it thoroughly and to separate the hackles. In between casts the fly can be re-dried by making one or two false casts in the air. The powder floatant is useful after a fish has been caught, when a little rubbed through the fly dressing will remove all traces of fish slime and perk up the hackles beautifully.

The leader tippet is extremely important to good fly presentation and should match the size of the fly. For flies size 14 the tippet material should not exceed 3x, for fly sizes 16–18 a 5x material is needed, and if smaller flies are used a 6x tippet will be necessary. These small-size tippets should not worry anyone, provided correct nylon knots are used, as the breaking strain of 5x nylon is sufficient to subdue most stream-bred brownies. It must be appreciated that nylon has an elastic quality that absorbs a lot of the action, and the rod tip also acts as a buffer against a fighting fish. However, be careful to watch for wind-knots in the tippet – these seriously weaken the nylon and a break is almost inevitable.

If the rise form is seen, the cast can be made to the feeding fish. The artificial should be cast diagonally up and across to a point slightly upstream of where the rise form was seen. A fish taking a natural does not only rise; the fact that it floats backwards has to be taken into consideration, and remember you seldom see a rise form until it has passed downstream of a feeding fish. After taking a fly a fish invariably moves back to its original position.

If your presentation is ignored, let your fly continue downstream before lifting it from the water, make a couple of false casts, then try again. Your first and second casts are your best chance of taking the fish. If you are unsuccessful it is better to move on and make a mental note of the lie for a future occasion.

The problem of drag has been left to last as it is the most important obstacle to be overcome when presenting a dry fly. It is practically impossible to present a dry fly, connected by a leader to a line, that will not be subjected to drag across the current. The best we can hope for is a free drift that is long enough to allow the fly to pass over the fish without hindrance. Many anglers do not appreciate this problem because they fail to see the signs of drag; they do not realise that the drag that is almost invisible to us is only too visible to the fish. No natural fly in free drift is ever subject to drag, and any unnatural behaviour by the artificial will instantly make the fish suspicious.

The curved cast to overcome drag has been discussed in Chapter 3. There are other ways to obtain a free drift – deliberately casting a wavy line is one of them – but each of these other methods results in a lot of slack line that will lose the fish by a delayed strike. The curved line is the most practical answer to the problem and should be practised until it can be properly performed.

Once you become proficient in the use of the dry fly new vistas open up. No longer need the wet fly be used when conditions dictate otherwise, and your bag will be considerably heavier as a result.

# Chapter 12

# *Lures*

It is extremely difficult to define the word 'lure', as all our artificial offerings are intended to lure the fish into taking them. We are no closer to a definition if we use the word 'lure' to describe all flies that make no pretence of imitating any known natural insect, because many small flies of traditional design come within this category. For our purposes, we really need to have two categories of flies (1) large flies that do not imitate any known form of life, but are tied with materials intended to attract, and (2) large flies that are intended to imitate small fish fry as bait.

The evolvement of lures on this side of the Atlantic has a background based on the pursuit of salmon and sea trout. Very little work has ever been done in the design of lures for coarse fish; it was believed that they were not suitable for the native brown trout. However, this is far from true. Not only will old cannibal browns take lures, but the use of a lure during early season is a splendid technique when fish are ravenous and building up their condition. During such times natural insect life is at a premium and a small fish fry simulator can be very tempting. For the past few years, lures have received a lot of attention from reservoir anglers fishing for stocked rainbow trout. In the early days of reservoir fishing the lures used were mainly sea trout flies, but today numbers of American patterns are used, and many more are home-designed.

On the American continent the evolvement of lures has been steadier and more progressive. From the beginning, the value of lures for all types of fish was realised and appreciated. The presence of a wider range of species probably had a lot to do with this, and so lures developed alongside the traditional flies.

### EDSON LIGHT TIGER

| | | |
|---|---|---|
| Hook | : | 10 or 12 long shank |
| Body | : | Peacock herl |
| Main-wing | : | Yellow hair (impala tail) |
| Secondary wing | : | Red quill feather |
| Tail | : | Amherst pheasant tippet |
| Tag | : | Flat gold tinsel |
| Throat | : | Yellow hackle fibre |

### EDSON DARK TIGER

| | | |
|---|---|---|
| Hook | : | 10 or 12 long shank |
| Body | : | Yellow chenille |
| Wing | : | Barred squirrel tail |
| Tail | : | Golden pheasant topping |
| Throat | : | Golden pheasant topping |

*Fig. 28 Lures*

New Zealand anglers were also pioneers of the lure technique, and many new patterns from that country are now known and used in the UK. New Zealand patterns mostly fall into the first category of our definition, and some of the methods used to tie these lures are unique. The Perch Fry shown in fig. 30, although my own design, is typical of New Zealand tying.

To be effective, a lure must either attract or deceive. The attractive qualities are shape, undulating movement, colour and flash, not necessarily in that order. To deceive, the lure must have the correct outline in the water, have convincing movement, possible flash, and imitate the colours of a fish fry. Lures in category (1) are of little interest to river-bred brownies, and are seldom effective. However, they most certainly interest perch, and sometimes small jack. Lures in category (2) are of interest to trout, perch and small jack.

Due to the literally hundreds of lure patterns on record, the selection for these pages has been most difficult, and has been restricted to those patterns which have an impeccable proven record. The country of origin has not been taken into account – the ability to take fish has been the criterion.

Probably the most outstanding lure in this category is the Edson Tiger, both the light and dark versions (see fig. 28). This lure originated in the USA many years ago, and has proved its worth against all species of fish, whether game fish, coarse fish or sea fish. On the North American continent it is tied in all sizes, depending on the quarry, but for our purpose sizes 10 or 12 are ideal for trout and perch.

The Edson Light Tiger should not be tied fat or bushy. It is a slim, streamlined fly, and when properly tied is quite elegant. The original pattern called for small pieces of gold tinsel to be tied-in as eyes, but this was discontinued many years ago and is now only seen in very old illustrations. I have tied this fly with small gold beads as eyes, and it certainly adds to the appearance, but it cannot be said that it made the lure any more attractive to the fish.

The Dark Tiger, although from the same stable, looks completely different from the Light one, and it is hard to think of the two versions as being the same lure. The differences are not a matter of outline and action in the water; in this respect they are both the same except for the predominant colour. So the Edson Tigers fall into both categories of our definition, they are attractors *and* deceivers, and consequently are equally effective for trout and perch. A large version, tied on a double hook with a pike trace, will also serve as an alternative pike lure.

The Thief originated somewhere on the western seaboard of Canada and the USA and there is considerable disagreement as to the correct tying, but the version shown in fig. 29 is widely accepted as correct. This lure, originally intended for wild rainbow trout, has a proven record of taking brown trout. It is a fish fry imitation and needs to be fished accordingly. This is a first-class lure for the early part of the season.

The Thor is a Canadian lure, and is definitely in the attractor class (see fig. 30). It is a simple lure with little embellishment, the attraction lying in the colour combination together with the flash of the polar bear wing. It has proved itself extremely

THE THIEF

| Hook | : | 12 (2x), bent to shape |
|------|---|------------------------|
| Body | : | Flat gold tinsel |
| Wing | : | Barred squirrel tail |
| Tail | : | Red quill feather |
| Head | : | Deer hair (spun Muddler Minnow style) |

*Fig. 29 Lure*

THOR

| Hook | : | 10 or 12 |
|------|---|----------|
| Body | : | Red chenille |
| Wing | : | White hair (preferably polar bear) |

PERCH FRY

| Hook | : | 10 or 12 long shank |
|------|---|---------------------|
| Body | : | Tying silk only |
| Side wings | : | Several golden pheasant tippet feathers tied-in so as to overlap |
| Tail | : | Red hackle fibres |
| Throat | : | Red hackle fibres |

*Fig. 30 Lures*

attractive to perch, but brown trout do not seem to be interested. Polar bear hair may prove very difficult to obtain in the UK, and there is no real substitute – ordinary white hair is a completely dead colour by comparison. If you know where some polar bear hair can be located, then try the Thor when fishing for perch.

The Perch Fry (see fig. 30) has been mentioned previously, and the origin may be of interest. During visits to a local reservoir, I noted many occasions when small fry were being pursued into the shallows by larger fish. The commotion caused was unmistakable; the shallows would boil with the activity. It was believed that large rainbows were chasing the perch fry which were present in vast numbers. I decided to have a go for these fry-eating cannibals, and after considerable experimentation at the tying bench, the golden pheasant tippet feather was selected as the best material for the lure. The problem was how to use it, and this was finally overcome by using a similar tying to the New Zealand Mrs Simpson lure.

It is said that the proof of the pudding is in the eating. The lure proved of no interest to the rainbow trout, but the first time it was used it took the two largest perch I have ever caught! On later occasions it was found that the larger perch were the predators causing all the commotion, the resident rainbows keeping very clear of the chase. Time and again the Perch Fry lure has proved its ability to attract large perch, and this odd-looking fly is worth having in your fly box.

The Minnow (see fig. 31) is a standard fish fry imitation, and can be used in various colour combinations throughout the season. The colours shown are the most common, but the lure may also be dressed with a brown upper-wing or a yellow under-wing; on occasions a combination of green and brown have worked quite well. This lure is particularly effective against early season browns and will sometimes take browns when the water is on the high side and coloured, and will always be of interest to the perch. The painted eye should never be omitted – it is the predominant feature of this lure, the sparse hair wings only giving a wraith-like outline under water.

The Mickey-Finn lure (see fig. 31) has a most interesting background. Both Canada and the USA have claimed the origin of this pattern, and certainly it was publicised and named by a

MINNOW

| | | |
|---|---|---|
| Hook | : | 10 or 12 long shank |
| Body | : | Flat silver tinsel |
| Top wing | : | Black hair (impala tail) |
| Under wing | : | White hair (impala tail) |
| Tail | : | Red hackle fibres |
| Throat | : | Red hackle fibres |
| Head | : | Black-painted eye |

MICKEY-FINN

| | | |
|---|---|---|
| Hook | : | 10 or 12 long shank |
| Body | : | Flat gold tinsel |
| Wing | : | Hair – yellow over red over yellow |
| Tail | : | Red hackle fibres |
| Head | : | Red hackle fibres |

*Fig. 31 Lures*

sports broadcaster over Canadian radio many years ago, but it was at a New York Game Fair that it was really brought to the attention of the angling public. The lure was an instant success, and although many years have passed since that Game Fair, it is still rated a top lure today. Part of its original attraction was the unique way it was tied, and the original pattern is well worth describing.

Everyone who has ever pulled apart the fibres of a quill feather knows how easily they can be 'married' together by smoothing with the fingers. Each fibre has minute hooks along the edge that grip the next fibre. The fact that feather fibre could be 'married' in this way was the basis of the Mickey-Finn. The upper wing of yellow over red over yellow was made up with slips of dyed swan quill feather, 'married' together by smoothing with the fingers, then tied in as a single unit. The result was probably the most exquisite fly ever seen: pure art. The pattern itself proved to be a real killer for brook trout, and the firm of Fin, Fur and Feather Ltd of Montreal, Canada, produced thousands of these lures to satisfy the tremendous demand.

When it was realised that the lure could also be tied as a 'bucktail', using coloured hair for the wing, the demand on professional tiers diminished and Mickey-Finns were produced at the home bench. It was inevitable that the wing would be replaced by hair, for in use the original lure soon became tatty and hair-like anyway. The substitution of hair for the wing made no difference to the killing capabilities of the lure, and today it is very rare to see the Mickey-Finn tied the original way. However, as a flytying exercise, or as an entry for a flytying competition, the original pattern is well worth trying.

The Mickey-Finn has proved almost useless for brown trout, but it does have a certain attraction for rainbows. It is when it is used against perch that its value to anglers becomes apparent – it has very few equals as a perch lure. When tying this lure, difficulty may be experienced in keeping the colours of the hair wing neat and separate. An explanation and illustration of a novel method to achieve this separation will be found in Chapter 16 fig. 39.

If the reader takes an interest in lures and searches out new patterns to try, it will not be long before the terms 'bucktail' and 'streamer' cause considerable confusion. Originally all such lures were tied with either bucktail wings (the 'bucktail'), or with wings of quill feather or complete hackle feathers (the 'streamer'). Today, although bucktail is still sometimes used, it is more usual to find these lures tied with finer hair. Impala tail is very popular – but they are still called 'bucktails'. Quill feather is now very rarely used, but a pair of hackle feathers make an admirable wing with plenty of undulating movement under water; feather wing lures are usually described as 'streamers'.

## Fishing the lure

It is only too easy to fish the lure as if it were an oversize wet fly, and this is completely contrary to the basic concept of lure fishing. If the lure is to be effective, it cannot be cast and retrieved as if a spinning outfit were being used. Lure fishing calls for its own technique, especially in running water, and the technique does not vary regardless of whether lures from groups (1) or (2) – previously described – are used.

The angler who at one time or another has fished a live minnow as bait is already familiar with this technique and will have little difficulty using lures. While I was staying at a renowned fishing lodge, situated on a strictly preserved 'fly only' water, every guest at the lodge was shocked when a group of three anglers – uninvited – suddenly descended on the river and commenced fishing with live minnows. Before the episode came to an end, the three strangers had half-filled a pillow-case with trout. As we watched their technique, a friend remarked: 'Moving about the stream like that, constantly pulling the line with their left hand, they look like berserk fiddlers who have lost their orchestra!' Maybe so, but when using a bait fish – or a bait fish simulator – it's the way to catch the fish. Have no doubt, their methods were effective and their technique superb; we all should learn to fish our lures as competently.

As a first step, we should clear our minds of wet fly technique, and look upon the lure as a fish fry simulator; even lures in the attractor class need to be thought of in this way. It must be borne in mind that, although a perch may take an attractor lure because of its colour or flash, it is still taken because it represents something alive and moving. Of course, there are times when such a lure is taken out of pure aggression, but the act of aggression is still made against what is presumed to be a living thing, and small living things are edible.

Our first requirement from a lure is movement. There are two types of movement: (a) the movement imparted by the manipulations of the angler, and (b) the movement made underwater by the materials with which the lure is tied. The (a)-type movements – the darting to and fro, the rise to the surface, the skipping action across the surface, the swim across current – may be imparted by the manipulation of the line and the rod tip. The (b) type of movement is far more subtle; during moments of pause in the retrieve the materials should continue the movement by undulating and pulsating in the current. Hair wings are excellent in this respect, especially if tied-in very sparse. Tinsel bodies result in 'flash' that gives the impression of movement, even when they are not moving. Just because a lure has a body of herl or chenille it must not be assumed that it lacks 'flash'. The herl or chenille traps microscopic bubbles of air that glisten under water, while at the same time showing an indistinct outline.

The second requirement is for the lure to 'work' where the fish are likely to be, and here we must rely on river craft and our ability to 'read' the water. We do not need long retrieves. We can take a leaf out of the minnow-fisher's book, neatly cast the lure into all likely lies and holes, then manipulate it so that its movements, both (a) and (b), are attractive to any nearby fish. Fast and short pulls on the fly line, in conjunction with rod tip movements, will impart an irregular action to the lure. The current should be completely ignored and not used to manipulate the lure in any way. The technique of 'free drift' has no place in effective lure fishing. Do not waste too much time on any particular spot – keep moving on to fresh fish.

Another good technique, especially for early season trout, is to use a weighted lure and cast upstream of a likely hole. Allow time for the current to carry the lure into the hole and for it to settle on the bottom. It never hurts to give extra time to make sure the lure is well in the hole, and deep. The retrieve should then be extremely fast and erratic – try to bring the lure right up to the surface without any pause. Once the lure has reached the surface, if it has not been taken, continue the retrieve until the lure is well away from the hole. In this manner very little disturbance is created and the hole may be tried again before moving on.

One last point about fishing the lure. Never try to fish a lure on a fine tippet. It is completely unnecessary and will lead to all sorts of complications. All of the lures mentioned, even when lightly weighted, are ideally suited for presentation on 3x nylon – use 2x if fish of over 1.2 kg (2½ lb) are expected.

## Chapter 13

# *Terrestrials*

As the fishing season progresses into the summer months the diet of fish becomes more varied and terrestrials begin to form a major part of their food, and by mid-summer probably the most important part. It would be difficult to over-emphasise the importance that should be placed on this aspect of flyfishing. Many anglers are well aware of these facts, but very few take an active interest in the presentation of terrestrial imitations.

The course of a river through the land makes it inevitable that small land creatures, terrestrials, will find themselves accidentally on, or in, the water. The list is a long one – worms, slugs, snails, ants, beetles, caterpillars, grasshoppers, and many types of terrestrial flies – and they all represent food for the fish. A few of these creatures are, by tradition, not suitable for imitation – not being in the insect category – but many others are well suited to our purposes and should not be neglected.

Many years ago Vince Marinaro wrote *A Modern Dry Fly Code* (Crown Inc., New York, 1950) – a very important introduction to fishing with terrestrial imitations – and since then more work has been done. Many new terrestrial patterns have been introduced. (See my book *Trout and Terrestrials*, published by Swan Hill Press).

There exists an exciting challenge to the flytier's art. These creatures are so varied in appearance that all our ingenuity is required to produce killing imitations. How rewarding it is to persevere until an artificial is produced that is taken as readily as the natural – a personal satisfaction that is hard to describe.

Ants of all sizes, both black and brown, winged or otherwise, are all readily taken by the fish. Sometimes the phenomenon

ANT

| | | |
|---|---|---|
| Hook | : | 10, 12, 14, or 16 long shank |
| Body | : | Two segments of body plus head are built up with black tying silk, then given several coats of lacquer until glossy |
| Hackle | : | Black |

NIGHT MOTH

| | | |
|---|---|---|
| Hook | : | 10 or 12 long shank |
| Body | : | Deer hair (spun Muddler Minnow style) clipped very short |
| Wing | : | Duck or teal breast feather fibres |
| Hackle | : | Brown – tied palmer |

*Fig. 32 Terrestrials*

occurs of a 'slick' of ants carried downstream by the current, all semi-sunk in the surface film and very difficult to see. The number of rises to the near-invisible 'slick' is often the only indication the angler has of their presence. Fishing with an ant imitation can be rather exasperating; many anglers obtain excellent results, while others have long given up trying. I have tried many patterns, in many colours and sizes, all with poor results, but I am still persevering. The best results so far have been obtained with the pattern shown in fig. 32. It is an easy pattern to tie, even in the smaller sizes, and sinks very nicely into the surface film. It can be improved by substituting black acetate floss for the tying silk – the acetate floss semi-dissolves when it is lacquered with acetate varnish, and subsequent coats of the acetate create a translucent effect.

The daddy-long-legs or crane fly is always appreciated by the fish, and is an excellent fly in late summer when the natural is abundant. Fished as a wet fly in free drift, it is often more readily taken than a standard wet fly or nymph. The pattern shown in fig. 33 is a new one; the body is much longer and slimmer than other patterns, and this has proved more acceptable to the fish. The body of the natural insect is extremely long and thin, and some of the standard imitations on offer look nothing like the real thing.

The Drone Fly (fig. 33) may be used to represent the large tribe of terrestrial flies that have yellow-and-black striped bodies. These naturals do not find their way onto the water that often, but whenever they do they are greedily taken. Until now the American pattern, the McGinty, has been used as the standard artificial – and for good reason, it's a proven killer – but I have had excellent results with my Drone Fly. The method of dressing is similar to that of the ant, except that two colours of silk are used, and the repeated coats of cellulose varnish give it a very lifelike appearance. Acetate floss cannot be used as the colours would disintegrate. It is usual for this fly to be fished as a 'dry fly', semi-submerged, and used to search out all likely shaded lies. Under these conditions the McGinty is inclined to become

DADDY-LONG-LEGS

| | | |
|---|---|---|
| Hook | : | 12 or 14 extra long shank |
| Body | : | Strands of deer hair bound along hook and shank to beyond the bend, cut off square |
| Wings | : | Brown hackle points |
| Legs | : | Pheasant tail fibres knotted, tied-in so as to lie straight back |
| Hackle | : | Brown |

DRONE FLY

| | | |
|---|---|---|
| Hook | : | 10, 12 or 14 long shank |
| Rear body | : | Built up with black and yellow tying silk, then lacquered until glossy |
| Front body | : | Built up with black tying silk, then lacquered until glossy |
| Hackle | : | Brown |

*Fig. 33 Terrestrials*

quickly waterlogged, and before very long is performing as a wet fly. The Drone Fly tends to remain floating in the surface film.

Caterpillars, both green and black, are excellent takers of fish that lie under overhanging foliage. Trout love them and chub are often interested in the larger sizes. During the summer months, many caterpillars fall to the water from overhanging branches, and what appear to be dormant fish quickly take them. It is usually better to cast directly to such lies rather than float the artificial down to them; in this way the fish will see the caterpillar land on the water in a natural way. Be prepared for the artificial to be taken immediately it alights on the water – a tightened line and you should be connected. The imitation caterpillars shown in fig. 34 have proved their worth and will serve you well.

Whenever the various moths land on the water they are much appreciated, particularly by the larger fish. Moths are essentially nocturnal insects, active at dusk and throughout the night. No matter how dark, there is always some light, and what light there is reflects from the water surface. It is probably this reflection that attracts the moths to the water and they attempt to settle against the reflected light in the same way as they would against a lighted window pane. They are seldom trapped by the water, their strong legs and wings enabling them to become airborne again as they skitter across the surface.

The take-off from the water surface is very similar to the actions of a sedge fly, the insect leaving a wake behind that is clearly visible even in the poor light. The fish seem to sense that their prey is about to escape and the result can be a noisy slashing rise that is quite savage.

Quite often, at dusk, we are faced with no appreciable hatch of aquatic flies, and although some fish are rising to midges, there is little other activity. The imitation moth is the complete answer to such conditions. It has the advantage of being large and easily seen, and any drag we set up will work to our advantage, appearing quite natural.

GREEN CATERPILLAR

| Hook | : | 10 or 12 extra long shank |
|------|---|---------------------------|
| Body | : | Light green chenille |
| Head | : | Peacock herl |

BLACK CATERPILLAR

| Hook | : | 10 or 12 extra long shank |
|------|---|---------------------------|
| Body | : | Black ostrich herl |
| Head | : | Peacock herl |

*Fig. 34 Caterpillars*

If you wish to extend dusk fishing until the light has gone completely a moth imitation is probably the best fly to use. Fine terminal tackle is not needed; a 2 m (7 ft) leader with a 3x tippet will serve very well.

After an evening's fishing, some friends and I often used to sit on the bank chatting to pass the time until it was dark enough to put up a good-sized moth imitation. A half-hour spent casting the moth, then activating it with short retrieves across the surface often produced the best fish of the day.

The moth pattern shown in fig. 32 is intended to represent a general pattern for all moths. Colours can be varied – white is excellent for a night moth – but the general outline should be retained. Various body materials can be used, but close-clipped spun deer hair is by far the best. It is essential that the moth artificial is a good floater and will not become waterlogged as it is manipulated on the surface. Spun deer hair is very buoyant and lightweight, and makes a most natural-looking body.

In spite of the disparity in sizes, we should couple midge fishing with use of the moth, for they are usually both on the water at the same time. The 'midge' is not a particular fly – some are aquatic, most are terrestrials attracted by the humidity of the water; the term applies to a multitude of very small flies, many minute. True imitation is out of the question – even flies tied on size 24 hooks are far too big. However, fish feeding on midges are taking a variety of these small insects, not all of them the same size, colour or shape. An extremely small artificial will often be accepted with the rest. The Black Gnat, shown in fig. 27 is a good pattern for this type of fishing, but the hook size should be size 20 or smaller. These very small offerings require an extremely fine tippet for correct presentation; nylon in the category of 5x or 6x needs to be used. The breaking strain of such nylon, after knotting, is a little over 226 g (8 oz), so a great deal of care is needed in playing a good fish. This should not frighten anyone off midge fishing, the small hooks hold very well and 5x nylon – helped by its elasticity and the rod tip – is surprisingly resilient. Midge fishing is a lot of fun!

Beetles form a major part of the fish's diet, a much greater part than is generally realised. Many anglers fishing a wet fly have caught fish on an imitation beetle, for many wet flies give an excellent impression of a beetle – some, in fact, were designed with that purpose in mind. The Alder, the Coachman, the Black Spider and Peacock Spider are typical of wet flies in this class. The Welsh regional wet fly, shown in fig. 18 is an excellent imitation of the many small beetles that abound in the Welsh valleys. However, beetles come in all shapes and sizes, and the larger ones, so appreciated by the big fish, cannot be adequately represented by wet flies. After falling on water the beetle very quickly drowns, and no manipulation by the angler is necessary to impart action to the artificial. Some years ago it was noted that drowned beetles invariably released their wings so that they spread out behind them; if an artificial is tied this way it can only add to the attraction, but beetles tied without extended wings are also quite readily taken.

The pattern shown in fig. 35 is a general pattern that can be tied in all sizes. Fig. 40 shows in detail how the deer hair is

BEETLE

| | | |
|---|---|---|
| Hook | : | 10, 12 or 14 long shank |
| Underbody | : | Tying silk only with black hackle tied palmer – then hackle trimmed short on top |
| Overbody | : | Pheasant tail fibres tied in to bend, brought back to head and three coats of lacquer applied |
| Head | : | Black tying silk |

The Beetle viewed from above

*Fig. 35 Beetle*

handled during the tying process. Legs may be imitated as shown in fig. 35 by a hackle-wound palmer, or the deer hair ends may be left extended at the head, as in fig. 40, both methods of tying being acceptable to the fish.

Once the artificial beetle has been tied, the back should receive several coats of clear varnish until it is smooth and glossy. In use, the artificial cannot be controlled as to which way up it lands on the water, but it does not matter, the fish show no preference.

The artificial beetle should be fished as a semi-submerged dry fly, paying particular attention to avoiding drag. Cast to likely lies under overhanging foliage, especially those areas in deep shade. Many of those lies are very difficult to reach with an upstream cast because of overhanging foliage touching the water. Such conditions can be overcome by floating downstream and paying out line, but drag is nearly always present. I overcome such drag by a novel way of paying out line – as fast as line is stripped from the reel with the left hand, it is fed through the rod rings by holding the rod horizontally and flicking the rod tip from left to right. The resulting 'snakey' line on the water minimises drag at the fly. It will not negate the drag – there is no way to accomplish that – but it does help the situation considerably.

There are many more terrestrials that have not been covered. It is hoped that in the future many more patterns will be designed as more and more anglers realise the importance of terrestrials. The so-called 'dog days' of summer are only in the imagination; the proficient user of terrestrials has good fishing through the whole season.

# Chapter 14

# Hooking, Playing and Landing

Before we can consider hooking a fish, it is necessary to take a look at the hook itself. Today, there are many manufacturers producing a bewildering array of hooks in a multitude of designs. Some of the latest advances in hook manufacture have little bearing on the angler's needs, and what are presented as scientific breakthroughs are, in fact, little more than new manufacturing techniques. The angler's needs are basically simple; he needs a strong hook correctly formed, of good temper and size, of correct weight, and with a barb of the right shape and sharpness.

Let us review these features one at a time. A good hook needs to be formed with a forged bend even when the lightest hook wire is used in manufacture, as this is the weakest part of the hook and the most vulnerable to breakage. The temper of the hook wire should be such that, when the hook is placed in the tying vice and the shank flicked with the finger nail, a decided 'spring' is detected. The hook must be available in a weight that suits its intended use – lightweight for dry flies, heavier wire for wet flies and lures. The barb, the most important part of the hook, must be small and distinctly formed with a sharp point.

The barb needs more consideration than it normally receives. Under ideal conditions a barb is totally unnecessary – in fact, it hinders hooking, because extra pressure is needed for the hook to penetrate beyond the barb. As ideal conditions require a constant tight line with never a fraction of slack (a condition that rarely exists), a barb is used to make the hook more secure in the fish. It therefore follows that the smaller a barb can be made, consistent with holding power, the better.

Hooks direct from the manufacturer are seldom as sharp as they can be made by the angler himself. All hooks benefit from a light touch with a sharpening stone, and a good time to do this is before the hook is placed in the tying vice. Once the fly is in the flybox it will need constant inspection and the occasional touch with the sharpening stone – this is especially true in the case of wet flies where slight rust may occur. When sharpening a hook, be sure to sharpen the inside of the barb only, and stroke the stone towards the point. This will cause the end to point outwards and increase the hook power.

The length of the hook shank has a direct bearing on the penetrating power of the point; the longer the shank the greater the pressure exerted on the point. In most cases the length of the shank is determined by the fly to be tied on the hook, but whenever possible 2x long shanks (twice standard length) should be used. Wet flies present no difficulty in this respect, but many dry flies are out of all proportion if tied with such elongated bodies. One way to overcome this problem is to tie the fly on the rear three-quarters of the hook shank, leaving a small portion of the shank protruding beyond the finished head. The effectiveness of the fly is in no way impaired – in fact, its balance is improved.

Hooks are available with a variety of bend shapes, but for flyfishing small streams we only need to concern ourselves with two of these; the round bend and the sneck bend. Without doubt the sneck bend has superior hooking power over the round, but the disadvantages of using the sneck bend are numerous. Quite apart from the flytying difficulties, the balance of a small fly is badly disturbed by the poor weight distribution. Wet flies tend to swim on their sides with rather a peculiar motion, and dry flies often fail to 'cock' beautifully on the surface. The river angler cannot go far wrong if all his flies are tied on round-bend hooks.

The size of hook is determined by the size of the fly to be tied on it. It is a complete fallacy that larger hooks will hold the fish more securely; the average stream trout is securely held on any hook between size 20 and size 10. Elsewhere in these pages, reference has been made to the dismal practice of tying flies of the same size on varying hook sizes, in the erroneous belief that they represent different sized flies. If the fly is required to be small, the hook size must correspond to it – hooking power does not enter the equation.

It is appreciated that not all anglers tie their own flies, but the foregoing should still be the criteria demanded of shop-bought flies. That a fly comes from a professional tier is no guarantee that it will meet the requirements of a discerning angler; the hook on which the fly is tied is a very cheap part of our tackle – but probably the most important part.

Before we consider the playing of a fish, we should clearly establish in our minds what we are attempting to accomplish. A fish is 'played' to enable it to be taken from the water, which cannot be done immediately it is hooked for two reasons. First, although the fish is almost weightless in the water, its struggles plus the weight of the water itself are normally enough to break the fine tippet at the end of the cast. Second, the same struggles and water weight tend to tear the hook from the hold it has taken. By playing the fish we are able to subdue its struggles to the point where it can be drawn over the net, or to the hand, without the risk of breakage or the hook tearing out.

The above may sound elementary, but it is surprising how many anglers take the words 'playing a fish' literally, and derive a great deal of pleasure letting the fish run wherever it wants while they 'play with it'. Not only is this extremely bad sportsmanship, but gives no thought to the well-being of the living creature. Perhaps we might be better off if we used the words 'subduing the fish', instead of 'playing'.

A trout should always be removed from the water as quickly as possible, consistent with avoiding breaking the tippet or tearing out the hook. To accomplish this we must, from necessity, be prepared to let it have line, but we should contest every inch of line we give. With smaller trout it is always best to 'handline' rather than play the fish from the reel, but larger and heavier fish are best controlled direct from the reel. The ratchet of a reel seems to create erratic behaviour in the fish – perhaps the vibrations are carried down the line. The ideal reel is ratchet-free when giving line, drag being maintained by a slipping clutch. This point should be borne in mind when a new reel is purchased. Such reels are readily available and any good tackle dealer can advise on this. An alternative is to take the ratchet off and apply drag with the fingertips on the rim of the reel.

To 'handline' a trout, the line should pass between the fore-finger and thumb of the hand holding the rod, and be drawn in or released by the other hand. If a light pressure is maintained between the forefinger and thumb, any slackness in the line will be kept to a minimum. This is a very sensitive way to play a trout as every movement of the fish is clearly felt between the fingers, and is the ideal way to handle all small-to-medium-size fish. The recovered line is just dropped at the feet until an opportune moment presents itself, when it can be reeled in. When fishing the dry fly upstream the dropped line presents no problem as it is carried downstream of the angler; when fishing a wet fly or lure downstream it is best to reel in slack from time to time.

The metabolism of a fish is geared for short bursts of quick activity, and prolonged expenditure of energy leads to complete exhaustion. If light pressure is maintained against it, and its breathing is restricted by the hook pulling the mouth open, it will tire quickly. Also, the initial burst of energy expended to escape the sudden restriction often upsets the swim-bladder (properly called the gas bladder), which will leave the fish unstable in the water. When the fish is almost played out it will roll towards the surface on its side, and if the head is then held above the water a further lack of oxygen will take its toll.

It must be appreciated that fish handled in the above manner will rarely recover if returned to the water – the injury and trauma are usually fatal. If the intention is not to kill the fish, or if it is under-sized, it should never be played out to this level.

Small fish can be drawn in quickly without fear of breakage, and larger fish should be netted as quickly as possible if they are to be released.

When playing a fish, only a light tension need be applied to the line. The struggles of the fish against the spring of the rod tip exert the main pressure, and this built-in 'spring' and the elasticity of the nylon cast act as shock absorbers against breakage. A rod held at a low angle, say 30°, exerts much more pressure than a rod held at a higher angle. Many anglers think that by holding the rod high throughout the fight they are applying maximum pressure – not so, the angle should be varied as needed.

Very often it is necessary to turn a fish that is running towards a bad snag. Use the rod to do this by lowering it to water level and applying side-strain to the fish. If the fish is large and cannot be safely turned in this manner then, sometimes, the giving of 0.9 m (1 yd) of slack line will do the job. It is possible that the fish, feeling no restriction, thinks the danger has passed.

A trout that has run into underwater vegetation is always a problem. It is almost impossible to dislodge such a fish by applying direct pressure, as the cast is probably wound round and round the tough stems of the vegetation. There are some standard remedies that can be tried – slack line can be given in the hope the trout will swim out of its own accord, or you can try tapping the rod butt while holding a tight line. The vibrations might induce the fish to move out or, more likely, swim deeper into the vegetation. Some anglers throw stones at the fish, but this is seldom effective. If the water can be waded, the best thing is to approach the weeds, reeling in the line, and try to release the trout by pulling the vegetation up. This is a real problem; only fortune will determine whether or not your cast remains unbroken.

After the fish has been played out it has to be landed, but before we discuss this in any detail let us take a look at the landing-net. Landing-nets have been briefly mentioned before, in Chapter 2 on tackle; here we are more concerned with their practical use. The river fisherman needs to carry a folding net that can be slung from his belt, bag or creel, and as we have already mentioned, the type that opens out to a triangle is by far the best. If it has an extending handle, so much the better.

The only other practical folding net has a solid hoop to hold the netting and, although this type of net folds for carrying, the round hoop remains rigid. No matter how this type of net is carried the hoop is an infernal nuisance to the wading fisherman, and it is not recommended.

The net comes into use at a critical juncture of our activities. Should it fail, the result will probably be a lost fish. For this reason the net must be considered as a vital part of the tackle, and looked after accordingly, lest it malfunction just when it is needed most. The mesh of the net itself should be examined frequently, its strength tested, and any small tears repaired. It is a good idea to tie a pierced lead bullet to the base of the mesh, one 13 mm (½ in) in diameter will do, as this will sink the mesh quickly in the water. The point where the side arms are hinged requires a little reel oil from time to time so that they will swing out easily with a flick of the wrist. When a net has an extending handle it is most important that this is lightly greased so that it slides freely. With attention paid to these points the net will function smoothly, and can be brought into action using only one hand.

The easiest way to net a fish is to unsling the net just before it is required, while the fish is a couple of rod lengths off. Sink the net in front of you so that it rests on the river bed, with the handle upwards against your body, or gripped between your knees. The played-out fish is then drawn towards you, head raised above water level, until it is over the submerged net. A smooth raising of the net will complete the operation.

A very useful tip is to trap the line with your forefinger against the cork grip of the rod as you draw the fish over the net, having first made sure that some line has been stripped off the reel and allowed to hang down. As soon as the fish is safely in the net release the trapped line. In this manner all tension is taken off the rod tip and the risk of breakage is kept to a minimum.

Should you fail to net the fish at the first attempt, don't panic; let the fish have a little line then repeat the procedure, taking care to make your movements smooth and deliberate.

If you have netted the fish properly, you will be left in the awkward position of a rod in one hand and a netted fish in the other, both connected by the line. If you are prepared to wade ashore this will present no difficulty, but if, as is so often the case, you do not wish to disturb the water, it is a different matter. To overcome this problem place the rod into the loops provided on most fishing waistcoats, hold the net handle firmly under your left arm and, using both hands, deal with the fish.

Whenever it is your intention to kill a trout, do so before you attempt to remove the hook. In the case of a small trout the easiest way is to insert the forefinger into the mouth, placing the thumb on the back of the head, and a hard backward bend of the head will kill the fish instantly. A larger fish will need a sharp rap on the base of the skull with a priest. Always kill a fish while holding it in the meshes of the net or you might lose it. The practice of banging the fish's head against the nearest stone is to be deplored – it is not only clumsy, it is cruel.

When handling fish that are to be returned to the water, always make sure your hands are wet and never squeeze the fish. If you hear a squeaking sound from the fish it means internal organs have been ruptured, and you must kill the fish instantly. Never, *never*, return a live fish by throwing it into the water; place it gently into the water with the head held facing upstream, and support it in that position until it swims away of its own accord. Always treat a captured fish with respect; it was a worthy adversary and deserves your full consideration.

# Chapter 15

# Spate Streams

Basically speaking, there are two types of stream, those that are rain-fed and those that are spring-fed. Of course, many streams are a combination of both types, or are fed by tributaries whose nature is different from the main stream. However, for the purpose of this discussion we only intend to consider the rain-fed stream, or spate stream as it is sometimes called. This type of stream is associated with the mountain and hill country of Wales, Scotland, the West Country and various parts of the North Country. Nearly all are excellent trout streams, although in many cases the trout are on the small side. Small they may be, but they are hardy fish and doughty fighters.

The average smallness of the fish is in most cases due to the acidity of the water and its inability to support food chains; and the lack of food due to the constant spates; and the lack of cover from their enemies. Regardless of their small size, these fish are well worth angling for. The skill needed to effect their capture is no less than that needed for larger fish, and we need our maximum skills to fish this type of water effectively.

An added bonus is the outstanding beauty of the scenery. No flat, featureless pastureland here, but cascading water down rocky gullies, beautiful rock pools and miniature waterfalls, often overhung by a canopy of trees in a densely wooded valley. All very beautiful, but testing water for the flyfisherman.

The course of the rain-fed stream has little respite from constant spates. Depending on the particular stream, these spates vary in intensity during and after periods of rain. Some streams only suffer a moderate rise in water level and a period of coloured water, while others become raging torrents of muddy water full of flotsam. The majority of streams are of a type between the two extremes, and considerably raised water levels can be expected, increased currents, and certainly coloured water.

This increased water flow may last only a few hours or may continue for days. The colour in the water, depending on the terrain, may be very temporary and clear long before the water level falls. The onset of the spate may be slow to appear, or almost instantaneous. I have experience of fishing a stream when there was a thunderstorm over the hills above. In less than an hour the rise in the water, plus the increased current, made wading most difficult, and the water was fast becoming an unpleasant browny-yellow.

These sudden changes in the water flow have a devastating effect on the trout's natural food supply. Underwater vegetation, the home of insect life, rarely gets established before it is swept away during the next spate. Small crustaceans, larvae and so on, are likewise swept away downstream. The stones and gravel of the stream bed are turned and scoured of all larvae attaching to them and, perhaps more important, are also scoured of algae which is part of the trout's food chain.

However, all is not lost. The spate also brings into the water many terrestrial forms of life, such as worms, grubs, beetles and other insects, and the trout have a gastronomical bonanza. But this food bonanza is short lived, and after the spate is over the trout resumes its search for normal food. It is at this point that the spate-induced shortage becomes apparent. Thus it is always 'feast or famine' depending on the rains, the overall effect being a general shortage of food, leading to an average small size.

Trout are, to a certain extent, creatures of habit; they find a good feeding station and make it their own permanent holt. To a trout, a good holt is one where it is largely sheltered from having to work against the current, where it is comparatively safe from predators, and where food is carried downstream to it in sufficient supply. Spates destroy these features by constantly scouring out banks and the stream bed, new prospective holts are formed and the trout have to relocate themselves. So life is hard on a trout living in a spate stream, but an equal number of problems are created for the angler.

It is of little use sitting on the bank waiting to match the hatch. True, there might well be the spasmodic hatch, but the tactical flyfisherman will spend most of his time prospecting for trout. Tactics will vary depending on the state of the water, and all types of flies will have to be used, wet, dry and terrestrial. Trout cannot be relied upon to be in the same holding positions as they were the last time the stream was fished. The stream bed will have changed during the last spate, depths will have altered and new holes been created. On each visit to such a stream the experienced flyfisherman will not rely on past experience of the water, but will read the stream anew with a practised eye.

Particular care will have to be exercised if, while fishing, a flash thunderstorm occurs, for it must be appreciated how temperamental such streams can be. To continue fishing with no thought of how to return to the opposite bank, or back to where a haversack or some essential piece of equipment has been left, would show a lack of common sense. The colour of the water needs to be watched constantly; changes in colour will occur even before the water rises and safe wading may become difficult. These small streams are full of holes that are just deep enough to slop water over the tops of waders, and when the water colours the stream bed soon disappears from sight.

When fishing such streams, the successful angler will be the one who is able to form a mental picture of many small fishing situations. In one stretch of water there lie hidden numerous features that would, on a larger river, constitute the main feature. The angler must be able to recognise them for what they are: a gravelly run may be only 0.6 m (2 ft) long, a pool may be only 0.3 m (1 ft) deep and extend between two rocks that are 0.3 m (1 ft) or so apart, a deep hole may be only 0.9 m (3 ft) deep with a surface area of a few square metres or yards. It is the ability to think in miniature that will bring the angler success.

Each of these features will require a different technique; tactics

131

must be changed every few yards, and only versatility will bring rewards. Unlike his fellow flyfisherman on a larger water, the small-stream angler will spend much more time over each stretch of water he fishes. Each nook and cranny must be searched out, the tactics and flies varied to suit each different feature encountered. It is virtually impossible to put up a favourite fly and fish your way up or down stream, and certainly not if you wish to be successful in taking those wild brownies!

Very often these tactics call for fishing with a very short line when presentation counts for far more than polished casting ability. We all like to think that we are able to cast a long, accurate line, but we must also learn how to fish a pool that might be only a short distance away – and to fish it with accuracy, stealth, and a thoroughness that will bring results. There will be times when the line hardly rests on the water and the cast is no more than a flick of the fly between two rocks. Very often no casting is required at all and the fly can be made to work its way from one feature to another. This is a true test of the flyfisherman's skills – and is immensely rewarding.

During periods of drought these streams are severely affected. What was once a reasonable trout stream now becomes a mere trickle over a course of sun-bleached stones. Most anglers shake their heads and leave the stream alone, but the trout are still there and waiting to be caught; it is up to us to find them. The technique is similar to that just discussed, except the situation has become even more miniaturised. There are still pools to be found – very small pools it is true, but still pools. There are still deep runs where the stream bed has been scoured out by a past spate, though these runs may now be shallow. Holes still exist under overhanging branches, even if now they are little better than deep puddles. Experience will enable us to spot such places, and skill will enable us to fish them successfully.

An incident is recalled when I took a 680 g (1½ lb) trout out of a shallow, isolated ditch, which at times of better water flow drained into the stream. This fish was in excellent condition and took a dry fly flicked onto the surface of the ditch.

So far we have considered the upper reaches of the spate stream; the lower reaches will need a different approach. Although still subject to spate, the lower reaches are usually wider and pass through a more level terrain and consequently are not so severely affected. In some cases the terrain is the floor of a wooded valley, in others it is moorland or pastoral – all bring their own specific problems.

A problem that is common to all is silt, and this can vary from a stream bed that is a mixture of sand and gravel to one that is, simply, muddy. More often, the lower reaches have sections of both types of stream bed. The disturbance of mud while wading is not necessarily a bad thing, kept to a minimum with little disturbance of the water, for it has the effect of stimulating the trout downstream. For instance, trout will often congregate below a cattle crossing in the sure knowledge that dislodged food items will be carried down to them from the disturbance. Most muddy stretches are also inclined to be placid and therefore offer themselves as possible dry fly water, and stream-bed disturbance will be of no consequence as one is fishing upstream.

Pastoral stretches invariably have high undercut banks, whereas moorland stretches invariably do not. High banks are a real problem to the flyfisherman, especially if wading is not possible. Remember, at all times keep off a high skyline where you are easily visible to the fish. High banks bring the added difficulty of casting without disturbance to water that is below your level. Casting a dry fly downwards with good presentation is something beyond the capabilities of most of us. Such situations really tax the ingenuity of the determined angler, for good fish are often found in pools contained by high banks. Each situation will call for its own solution; perhaps the wet fly can be fished on a long line, perhaps there are parts of the bank which can be partially descended, perhaps a convenient bush or tree can be used as concealment. Never rush into these situations without advance planning of tactics.

133

Open moorland stretches with low banks may also give problems if the water cannot be waded. Lack of cover must be overcome by keeping very low; kneeling while casting is always good practice in such situations. It has been suggested many times that the angler should crawl up to such water and cast from a prone position! This is not exactly an activity for the grey-haired ones – learning to cast a good line while kneeling is all that is required.

Fishing the lower reaches of a stream which cuts across the floor of a wooded valley is always a delight. Here there are probably all the features of the upper reaches without the severe miniaturisation. Anglers are able to practise their flyfishing 'properly' and bring their casting skills to the fore. Of course, streams through wooded terrain always bring casting problems, but a likely spot should not be passed up because of the danger of you losing a fly. Flies are the cheapest part of the tackle, and you must always be prepared to lose a few to get results. The best fish very often lie in places where casting is nigh impossible, so get into the habit of fishing such places and ignore the loss of a few flies.

An instance comes to mind where the branches of a tree so overhung the water that there was a separate water channel within the branches. A good trout could be clearly seen rising in the secluded channel and the only way to it was to cast a dry fly through a small gap in the branches. At first sight this was considered impossible, the gap was very small and called for an accuracy not usually exercised. Nevertheless, after the loss of three flies the trout was taken.

During this chapter we have come to one conclusion: to fish a spate stream efficiently requires the use of varied tactics. The importance of advance planning of tactics cannot be over-emphasised. These are delightful streams to fish, and their wild brownies a delight to pursue, but remember, only planned tactics will fill your bag.

# 16

# Fly Dressing
# Techniques

If the reader does not tie his own flies, and has no intention of
doing so, then that which follows may be of little interest.
However, even confirmed non-tiers have been known to change
their thinking, and perhaps the ways that certain special effects
are achieved may be of passing interest.

The instructions that follow are intended to elaborate on the
new fly patterns that have been introduced, some of which
require special techniques in their dressing. Some of these techniques may already be known to the reader; if not, you may
experience a little difficulty when attempting to tie certain of
these patterns which call for other than a standard fly dressing.
Many tiers have their own way of dressing a fly, and any way
is correct if it produces the required result – I do not want to
influence anyone's methods, only to give tips that might be
useful.

Herl-bodied flies, especially those of peacock herl, have been
in use for many years, but it is surprising how few of these flies
are well tied. Without doubt, herl laid onto the hook shank in
touching coils makes a beautiful-looking fly, but its wearing
qualities are just about nil. I hold philistine views where flytying
is concerned; a fly must not only look good, it must wear well
and be capable of taking many fish before it is finally discarded.
The three-strand method of dressing herl bodies (see fig. 36) not
only makes a fine-looking fly, but one which will take many fish
before it becomes unravelled. It is also ideal for large-bodied
flies such as the Edson Light Tiger shown in fig. 28.

135

Fig. 36 is largely self-explanatory, but a couple of tips may be useful. Before twisting the herls round the tying thread to form a 'rope', decide which way it is intended to wind the 'rope' onto the hook shank – clockwise or anti-clockwise. The herls must always be twisted round the thread the opposite way, otherwise they will become unwound during the tying. A light-coloured thread should never be used for this purpose – the finished result looks awful. If necessary, tie in a length of black thread just for this operation. A final tip – use unwaxed thread as a base for herl bodies.

While we are discussing the construction of fly bodies, it

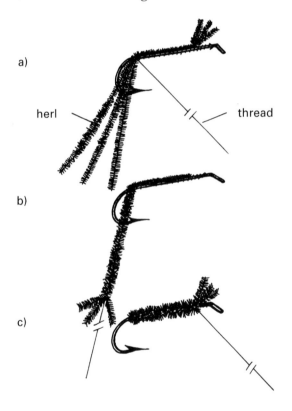

a)

herl

thread

b)

c)

*Fig. 36 Tying herl bodies*

might be as well to mention the blending of fur or hair for use as a dubbing material. It is well known that fur or hair of different colours can be blended together to arrive at the colour required, but it is a tedious business requiring much work teasing out the material between the fingertips. An easy way is to place the fur or hair – without cutting – in separate heaps of colour on a sheet of paper. Then feed the material, a little at a time, into a food blender (the type called a liquidiser). The spun material will clearly show the colour, and separate colours can be added until the required shade is obtained. After removal from the blender, the material can be chopped up to the consistency required for dubbing. Do not forget to clean up the blender afterwards – otherwise your use of it will be forbidden in future!

The use of chenille for fly bodies is not popular with flytiers, due to the bulky way it ties in on the hook shank and distorts the finished body of the fly. This problem can be overcome by stripping the end of a strand of chenille between the nails of the thumb and forefinger. The fibres will come away cleanly, leaving the twisted thread core of the chenille. Bind down the thread core onto the hook shank so that the actual chenille only commences at the bend. Before winding the chenille, place a small drop of varnish on the hook shank where the first turn will be placed – this will secure any loose fibres and strengthen the finished fly.

The black-and-yellow body of the Drone Fly (fig. 33) is simple and straightforward to construct, but the body of the American McGinty is a different matter. The McGinty pattern calls for a black-and-yellow striped body constructed of fine chenille, a specification which may be rather perplexing. The method of construction is shown in fig. 37, and is quite effective when completed. Unlike the hard, shiny Drone Fly, the finish is soft and furry. The strands of fine chenille, both black and yellow, are tied in together, then wound alternately on to the hook shank, each turn made trapping the colour of the previous turn. This chenille construction is an example where the above-mentioned method of tying in chenille is invaluable – the McGinty could not be tied without it.

Many patterns call for tinsel tags to be included in the dressing. The tag is an important ingredient of such flies, and should not be omitted because in the past such tags have become unravelled. Properly tied, there is no reason for any tag to become unravelled. By far the best material to use for a tinsel tag is Mylar tinsel, as it can be pulled very tight while winding round the bend of the hook, and is able to stretch sufficiently to follow the contour. However, regular tinsel will do a good job if it is handled correctly.

Always select a very narrow tinsel for a tag and bind it down for at least half the length of the hook shank. Commence the turns of the tag well before the bend of the hook and continue the turns one third of the way round the bend. The turns taken should be touching, not overlapping. On reaching the finishing point, continue the turns back towards the start of the windings, this time covering the join marks of the first turns laid down. Tie off by binding down for at least half of the length of the hook shank. The fly dressing can now be continued in the normal way.

Both tags and tinsel bodies of flies can be much improved if they are given a coating of clear lacquer. Only a thin coat should be applied, and this is best done with a dubbing needle. If it is considered necessary, further coats can be given, but always

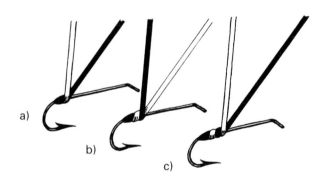

*Fig. 37 Tying a striped body*

wait until the previous coat is thoroughly dry. This lacquering operation must always be done immediately the tinsel is in place, never after the fly has been completed. No further tying should take place until all lacquer is completely dry. Be careful about this, for a lacquered body takes longer to dry than is generally thought. The lacquered tinsel will stay bright longer, will be more durable, and any uneven edges will be smoothed out.

There is usually very little difficulty experienced tying-in hair wings, but no matter how well they appear to be tied there always seem to be a few hairs that become loose, and after the loose ones fall out the rest quickly follow. There is no need for this difficulty to be experienced; it takes no more time to secure the hairs correctly (see fig. 38). Once the hairs are in position on the hook shank, take only two or three turns of tying silk round them, then either tie off or allow the thread to hang down on a bobbin. Before continuing, bend the hairs that point towards the eye back and upwards and cut off as shown (a). A small drop of head varnish should be placed on the cut ends and allowed to soak in (b), and while the varnish is still wet continue to tie-in the hair wing (c). Make sure to bind very tightly, biting into the wet varnish. A hair wing secured in this manner will never become loose during the life of the fly.

A common fault with many hair wing flies is that the wing becomes caught in the bend of the hook when the fly is used. Tying in the wing short is a very poor way to overcome this problem, as it destroys the design and balance of the fly and its intended action in the water. The fault lies in the way the wing was originally secured, a wing tied in parallel with the hook shank is bound to droop under the bend when it becomes wet. Whenever a hair wing is tied in, the last few turns of the thread should always be taken *under* the lifted wing, pulling the thread towards the eye of the hook so that the wing is secured in a slightly elevated position. When the fly is completed, there should be light between the lower hairs of the wing and the shank of the hook at the bend.

Several lure patterns call for multi-coloured hair wings, and it is of the utmost importance that the colours are kept completely separated, not tied in as a wing of mixed colour. The Mickey-Finn lure (fig. 31) is typical of this type of fly.

This problem is very easily overcome with the use of our old flytier's friend, Golden Gum. Fig. 39 shows the technique in detail. Once the hairs of a particular colour are selected, they are treated with Golden Gum. The best way to do this is to put the gum on the fingers and smooth it into the hair by rolling the hair between the fingers. Without waiting for the gum to dry

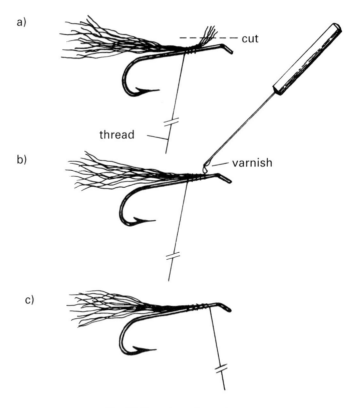

*Fig. 38 Securing a hair wing*

completely, the separate gummed ends can be easily tied in, if necessary one on top of the other.

When the tying-in is complete, tie off the thread with a couple of half-hitches or a whip finish so that it cannot become loose, then wash the fly under a running tap with warm water to remove all traces of gum. The fly can then be semi-dried by pressing it between the folds of a paper towel, and the tying continued. When this technique is used, the gum trapped under the bindings acts in the same way as the varnish in fig. 38. It must always be borne in mind that multi-coloured hair wing flies are very easily over-dressed. When added together, the multi-colours must not represent more wing than would normally be used of any one colour. It is surprising how few hairs of each colour are necessary to accomplish this result.

Another type of wing that sometimes gives difficulty is when duck or teal breast feather fibre is used as a material. These feathers have the most awkward curl in several directions, and the fibres vary enormously in thickness, even when taken from the same feather. This is the best way out of the difficulty.

Select a suitable feather, then smooth the fibres back from the centre stalk so that they stand out at a right angle. Carefully remove the soft, fluffy fibres from the base of the feather until only strong firm fibres remain, then remove sufficient of these fibres to create the wing required. Roll the fibres between the fingers to form a mixed bunch ready for tying in, totally ignoring the uneven lengths and the curl in the fibres. Tie in the wing in the usual way and, after the wing is securely in position, hold it tightly between the thumb and forefinger of the left hand while the uneven ends are nipped off using the nails of the thumb and forefinger of the right hand. Now complete the dressing of the fly. Finally, when the fly is completed, thoroughly wet the wing between moistened finger-tips until all fibres are straight and stuck together, then leave it to dry out naturally. When the fly has completely dried out, the fibres will be relatively straight without a pronounced curl, and the nipped ends will not be readily apparent.

Next, consider the painting of eyes on the heads of lures. The Minnow lure (see fig. 31) is one example of this technique. However, we must first discuss the preparation of the head to receive the eye, for without proper preparation the final result is impossible. Although in principle all heads of flies should be kept as small and neat as possible, in the case of heads to be painted with eyes a little leeway may be given. To be effective in the simulation of a fish fry, the eye must be large enough to be prominent with a good clear pupil, and this means that we must

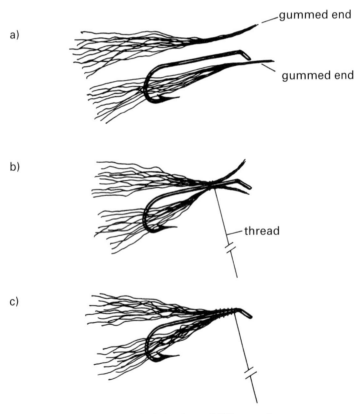

*Fig. 39 Tying in hair wings of different colours*

have a head large enough to take such an eye. The head must also be round and completely smooth to take the painting of the eye. A satisfactory eye cannot be painted onto uneven bindings, especially if minute fibres of the fly dressing protrude through the head whipping.

The first step is to be particularly careful to avoid forming an uneven head with any fibres trapped in the windings. With extreme care such fibres can be singed off with a lighted match – but with flammable materials close by this is a hazardous oper-ation that should be avoided if at all possible. Having obtained the head we require, finish with a whip knot and varnish in the usual way. Then, when the varnish is completely dry, apply a second coat of varnish using black cellulose. This is best done by holding the fly in the fingers and using a dubbing needle to run a small droplet of the black cellulose round the head. When it is completely dry, the head will look smooth and polished.

No attempt should be made to paint the eye until the head is absolutely dry. The first step is to use a dubbing needle to place a droplet of yellow cellulose on each side of the head. When dry, the droplets will have flattened out to nice, round eyes. Now take a matchstick and sharpen it to a blunt point, put a drop of black cellulose on a sheet of paper and dip the end of the match into it – a touch of the point of the match in the centre of each yellow eye will make the pupil. This may sound tedious, but it takes longer to describe than to carry out, and the finished result is well worth while.

Various types of dressing for the deer hair beetle have already been discussed, and all have one thing in common – the use of deer hair for the back of the beetle. Deer hair is ideal for this purpose; the hollow hairs are extremely buoyant and will float this rather solid fly easily. The general dressing of beetles should not give any difficulty, except that it is not easy to keep the back flat and wide at the bend of the hook. A very easy way out of this problem is shown in fig. 40. Before the deer hairs are bent back towards the eye of the hook, a needle is inserted over which the hairs can be bent. The needle can be left in place until the first coat of varnish to the back has dried, when the hairs will stay in place after the needle has been removed. It will take several successive coats of varnish to make the back nice and glossy.

It is well appreciated that other problems might arise during the tying of these new patterns, but flytiers are known for their ingenuity, and with a little thought all difficulties can be overcome. I am confident that many other better ways will be found to solve the problems already discussed. Flytying is a progressive art practised by those who appreciate a challenge.

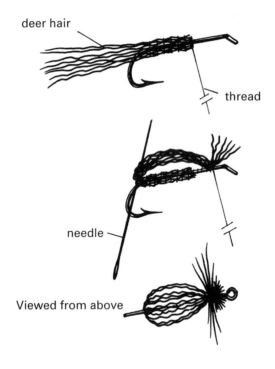

*Fig. 40 Construction of a deer-hair Beetle*

# Chapter 17

# *Nylon*

Whereas the anglers of yesteryear understood the gut they used for their leaders, took the precautions necessary, and obtained the best results possible from the substance, the anglers of today take nylon for granted. But nylon has as many peculiarities as the gut it replaced, and a thorough understanding of these peculiarities will result in an improved level of casting ability and, ultimately, more fish in the bag.

Nylon is basically a plastic product, man-made from extracts derived from coal, air and water. The nylon we use when fishing is produced by extrusion in a continuous single strand called a monofilament. It is translucent, almost colourless, and for all practical purposes may be considered almost invisible under water. It has no capacity to absorb water, and consequently water cannot cause rot, but over a period nylon deteriorates in bright light.

These facts could be classed as the advantages of nylon. Unfortunately, there are as many disadvantages. Nylon has a high tensile strength and takes a direct pull very well, but due to its method of manufacture it has an almost straight molecular structure and can be very easily damaged. Any bend or kink seriously weakens nylon. It is very easily abraded; it does not fray, but the tensile strength is affected and breaks occur. Nylon may also be classed as a semi-stiff, semi-brittle material, and has a definite tendency to set in hard coils.

The elasticity of nylon is a mixed blessing. It certainly helps us in the playing of a fish by acting as an additional buffer, but it adversely affects striking a fish, especially if the strike is at a distance, and the hook is large and needs to be driven home.

The weakness of nylon at any bend or kink, plus its tendency to 'spring' due to the semi-stiff composition, makes the use of special nylon knots an absolute necessity. There are many knots designed especially for nylon, but four knots – the needle knot, the blood knot, the half blood knot and the loop knot – will cover the majority of fishing needs. These four knots are shown in figs. 41 and 42, and although the illustrations are as clear as possible, they still look quite forbidding. The best way to learn these knots is to obtain a length of 3mm (⅛in) diameter nylon cord and practise until they can be performed easily – a pleasant enough pastime while sitting in a comfortable chair before the TV.

The needle knot is used to connect the butt of the leader to the flyline, or the tippet to the end of a braided leader. The blood knot, sometimes called a barrel knot, is the standard knot for joining together two strands of nylon. The half blood is an easy

Blood knot

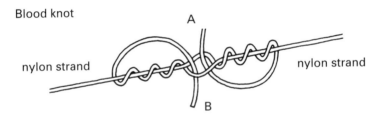

Half blood knot

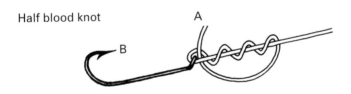

*Fig. 41 Nylon knots*

way to attach a fly to the tippet, and is quite secure provided that the tippet matches the size of the fly. The loop knot can be tied at the butt of the leader for connection to the flyline, but this is not recommended practice, and alternatives will be discussed later. A more practical use of the loop knot is to facilitate a quick change of tippet material. If an extremely small loop is tied half way along the tippet, new lengths of 0.45 m (18 in) tippet material can be added by using the half blood knot.

Nylon is produced in a number of different countries, some of

Needle knot

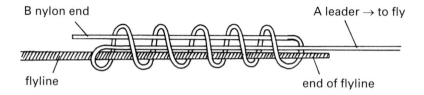

B nylon end                A leader → to fly

flyline                end of flyline

Loop knot

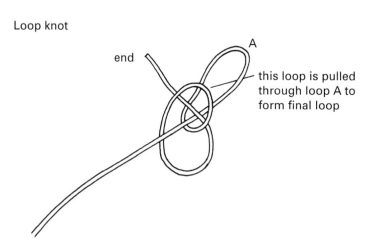

end

A

this loop is pulled through loop A to form final loop

*Fig. 42 Nylon knots*

147

which have earned a name for good nylon. France and the USA have excellent reputations. However, care is needed in this respect, for production techniques are changing all the time, and what was a good product for our purpose a few years back may be very different today. Examine any nylon most carefully before a purchase is made.

The qualities anglers require in nylon sound completely contradictory. The nylon should be hard, but we also need it to be limp. It must be strong, but at the same time we want the maximum breaking strain in the smallest diameter. Obviously, we have to be prepared to compromise. One warning must be given; the manufacturers' practice of grading their nylons by an 'x' number is highly unsatisfactory. The 'x' number may well give a fairly accurate indication of the breaking strain, but nearly all manufacturers produce a different diameter for each rating. True, we need to know the breaking strain, but we need to know the diameter much more, the reasons for which will become apparent later. Bear in mind also that the stated breaking strain does not apply to practical use in fishing; it is a measurement obtained in the laboratory, not under water. After knotting, all nylon will lose at least 30 per cent of the rated breaking strain.

Nylon may also be purchased in hard grades, soft grades, coloured, and treated to float or sink. Coloured nylon is of questionable benefit; the natural material is almost invisible under water and colour may only result in it becoming visible. Some nylon is produced that varies in colour along the length (usually green and brown). This may be more useful as it tends to break up the outline. There is little point to buying nylon pre-treated to float or sink, as this can be so easily done by the angler. In fact, if the leader has been permanently treated, it is a decided handicap to a quick change of tactics.

Diameter is very important to the angler for the simple reason that it is almost impossible to knot together two strands of nylon that vary more than 0.05 mm (0.002 in) in diameter, and still obtain a good strong knot. Although this fact is of paramount importance to the angler tying his own knotted leaders, it is equally important when varying tippets are knotted together. The manufacturers' 'x' number, as stated above, is of little help to overcome this problem. Many spools of nylon now carry the diameter as well as the 'x' number, and this is a considerable help, but far too much nylon is sold with only the breaking strain stated.

An ideal way out of this dilemma – but unfortunately available to only a few – is to measure the diameter with a micrometer and mark it clearly on each spool. The alternative is to keep to only one brand of nylon at all times, and to accept the descending 'x' numbers as an indication of which strands may be joined by knotting.

There is little doubt that the home-produced knotted leader is a very superior item and an absolute pleasure to use. It is a tiresome business, a lot of painstaking work is necessary, but very often it is a labour of love, and the result is very worth while. The shop-bought knotted leader cannot be compared with the hand-made version. Selected nylon carefully graded, plus hand-tied knots, produces a leader that cannot be duplicated by any machine.

Before we discuss the hand-made leader in detail, we should dispose of an old myth. Leaders *do not* have to be made out of stiff nylon. In fact, leaders of stiff nylon perform very badly, the turnover during the cast is unreliable and the final fly presentation is far from satisfactory. The fairly new braided leader is completely supple, yet it casts very well indeed, and we all know that a supple fly line improves casting – so it is hard to understand why anyone would want a stiff leader. The old belief that such a leader is desirable was probably due to the small-diameter butt sections that were at one time fashionable. It is now appreciated that the butt section needs to be at least 60 per cent of the diameter of the flying tip and, in consequence, we are able to utilise the advantages of limp nylon.

Not only must the butt section be of substantial diameter, it must also extend for at least 30 per cent of the leader. Sometimes this extended butt section is made up of two diameters, but the second strand is quite substantial.

Fig. 43 shows the design of two types of knotted leader. One is a gradual taper, the other is a steep taper. Both are 2.7 m (9 ft) long. The gradual taper is intended for use with large flies or lures, while the steep taper is preferable for dry fly presentation.

The final section of each leader represents the tippet, and needs to be a minimum of 0.6 m (2 ft) long. If a finer tippet is required it must take the form of an additional strand added to the existing leader, otherwise the step-down in diameter would be too great for satisfactory knotting. Of course, the original tippet may be shortened accordingly. Weighted flies may always have the tippet shortened, and very often the casting is much improved as a result.

Many years ago it was the custom to connect the leader to the flyline by means of a loop at the butt of the leader, and in fact many shop-bought leaders still have a loop at the butt end. The loop method of connection leaves a lot to be desired, as such loops rarely pass through the rod tip ring without snagging, and this usually happens just as a fish is being brought to the net. Even worse, the loop connection may pass through the rod tip ring, then snag as the fish suddenly takes more line. Our needs are much better suited by securing the butt end of the leader to the flyline by means of the needle knot (fig. 42) or, better still, by the use of a nylon cast connector (fig. 44).

Once a leader is permanently connected to a flyline there is the problem of storage. A leader that is wound onto a reel at the end of a day's fishing will give problems the next time out; it will have set into springy coils that are most difficult to remove. A nylon leader can be straightened by rubbing it between a folded piece of flat rubber, but this is rarely effective on coils that produce a spiralled leader. After fishing, wind the line onto the reel so that 150–200 mm (6–8 in) still protrude, then coil the leader into three or four loose coils of at least 300 mm (12 in) diameter. The reel can then be put into the reel case, the coiled leader remaining outside and separate. I have my own way of overcoming this problem. the leader is wound round the crown of my fishing hat – and the reel is stored in the hat!

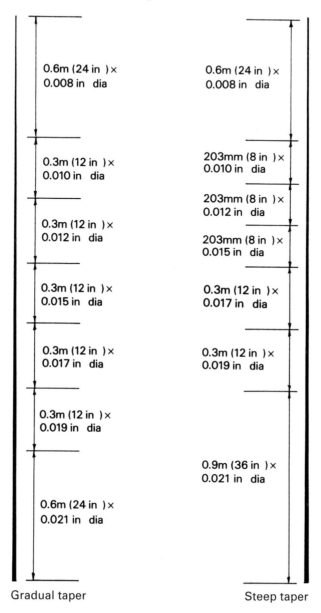

0.6m (24 in )×
0.008 in  dia

0.6m (24 in )×
0.008 in  dia

0.3m (12 in )×
0.010 in  dia

203mm (8 in )×
0.010 in  dia

203mm (8 in )×
0.012 in  dia

0.3m (12 in )×
0.012 in  dia

203mm (8 in )×
0.015 in  dia

0.3m (12 in )×
0.015 in  dia

0.3m (12 in )×
0.017 in  dia

0.3m (12 in )×
0.017 in  dia

0.3m (12 in )×
0.019 in  dia

0.3m (12 in )×
0.019 in  dia

0.9m (36 in )×
0.021 in  dia

0.6m (24 in )×
0.021 in  dia

Gradual taper

Steep taper

*Fig. 43 Knotted leaders*

151

Flyline                                      Leader

*Fig. 44 Cast connector*

It has been mentioned that nylon deteriorates in bright light and should therefore be stored under cover. Keep spools of spare nylon in a closed drawer, and spare leaders in some kind of cast wallet. Bear in mind too that season-long use in bright sunlight also takes its toll of leaders. It is a good practice to test leaders frequently by giving them a steady pull. Discard all nylon that is suspect, especially if any wind knots are found – never take a chance of losing that specimen fish!

# Afterword

It is inevitable that anything written on the art of angling will be controversial; the subject itself is highly controversial, but the effort must be made or foundations for future progress will never be laid. Many theories of the past have been expanded with the passage of time, but without that early work we would be sadly lacking in knowledge today.

Controversy is good for our sport, and it is our duty to future generations of anglers to expound our theories, even at the risk of these theories later being proved incomplete. It is the only route to progress.

Long after I have passed on to other waters, the angler of the future may regard these pages as antiquated. Nevertheless, if some foundation has been laid for future work, study and experimentation on new fly patterns, particularly terrestrials, it has all been very worthwhile.

Angling is much more than a sport. to obtain the maximum satisfaction from our interest it must become a life-long quest for knowledge, as many of the complexities of nature are hidden from us.

Eddie Bassin was fond of saying: 'When calculating the lifespan of man, the good Lord does not take into account the days spent fishing.' Let us hope Eddie was right, and resolve to spend the extra time allocated laying a solid foundation for the future.

# *Index*

154

pike *(continued)*
  mouth of  59–61
  size of  59
  trace for  61
  weight of  59
Plecoptera  85
Pleuroptera  85
polarised sun-glasses  20

reel  16, 17
  size of  17
  weight of  17
reel seat  16
Reflector Nymph  73, 75, 76
rod handle  16
rod rings  16

sedge  85
short line fishing  132
silver sedge  86
smuts  85
spinner  84
split-cane  15
stream bed  133
  mud  133
  silt  133
sub-imago  84

tags  138
terrestrials  113, 130
  ants  113, 114
  beetles  113, 119, 120, 121

caterpillars  113, 117, 118
Diptera flies  113, 115, 116, 119
grasshoppers  113
moths  114, 117, 118
slugs  113
snails  113
worms  113
thunderstorms  131
tinsel  138
Trichoptera  85
trout  35
  age of  36
  brown  35, 39
  colour of  36
  eyesight of  37
  feeding stations  41
  hearing of  36
  rainbow  35, 39

waders  20, 21
wet flies  67
  colour of  69
  materials  72, 73, 74
  parts of  68
  regional  70
  size of  75
  storage of  76
  types of  71
  weighted  71, 72
willow flies  85

yellow mayfly  85